# Virgin Islands
# COOKING

**by Carol Bareuther**

American Paradise Publishing, St. John, USVI

**This book is dedicated** to the hundreds of Virgin Island cooks who tirelessly helped me during its creation. I am honored to have received so much kind assistance from so many wonderful people over the years. I am not sure which I enjoyed most during this project––sampling the cooking or meeting the chefs! Both are national treasures. Thanks again.

**(ISBN 0-9631060-6-6)**

**Publisher's Note**: The contents of this book is copyrighted 1994 by Carol Bareuther. None of this material can be reproduced in any way without written permission from the publisher. Contact American Paradise Publishing at: Box #37, St. John, VI 00831-0037 Telephone and fax (809) 693-8876 or Answering Service 776-6922. Special thanks to Keryn Bryan and Kate Norfleet of KATYDIDS DESIGN for the cover art, and Lani Clark for services rendered.

**American Paradise Publishing, St. John, USVI**

# TABLE OF CONTENTS

## INTRODUCTION

The cuisine of the Virgin Islands is as rich, vibrant, and culturally diverse as its inhabitants. Our local chefs are, quite rightly, renown throughout the Caribbean——and the entire world, for that matter——for their imaginative culinary skills. There are good, solid reasons for this.

The most important reason is the ethnic diversity of our sun-kissed islands. Traditional West Indian cooking is actually an artful combination——a tasty melting pot, if you will——of various Amerindian, African, East Indian, Asian, and European cooking styles.

Long before Columbus set foot on our sandy shores in 1493, Ciboney, Arawak, and Caribe Indians exchanged recipes, borrowed ingredients, and swiped spices from one another.

With the arrival of Columbus came all the rich flavors of Europe; the native dishes of the France, England, Holland, Denmark, Portugal, and Italy literally washed ashore with his crew.

Then the Africans arrived and began to share '...a pinch of dis and a handful of dat.'

Each of these various cultures brought something unique to the culinary table——a different method of cooking, or a new spice, or another way of preserving food.

Soon the newly arrived cooks began to incorporate more and

more tropical plants into their dishes. Spicy new herbs suddenly added zest to their traditional main dishes.

There was an explosion of cooking experiments. Recipes incorporating local foods and spices were eagerly traded.

Local fish were hooked, netted, and speared—and then roasted, baked, and fried over an open fire. Whelks, conchs, and snails were cooked in a number of different ways. Coconut palms were used for food, drink, medicine—and a million-and-one other things.

The contemporary result is a glorious mix of African, English, French, Spanish, and Indian dishes which we now call Caribbean cuisine—or more properly, Creole cuisine.

Of course, this did not start with Columbus. He was a late-comer on the scene. Long before the birth of Jesus Christ, the primitive Ciboney Indians migrated northward through the Lesser Antilles from South America. They traveled in ocean-going canoes, and were hunters, fishermen and explorers.

Approximately a thousand years ago, the peaceful Arawaks followed in their watery wake. The Arawaks brought with them their favorite dietary staple, the cassava root. They used cassava in a wide variety of imaginative ways—as a vegetable and a flavoring—but most importantly, to make bread.

Local archaeologists still occasionally unearth ancient 'griddle' stones which the Arawaks used while making their cassava bread. And today our local restaurants still feature sweet cassava bread and a spicy meat stew called pepperpot, which is flavored with cassava-based cassareep.

The Arawaks incorporated such Caribbean foods as allspice, red chili peppers and guavas into their diet. They were skillful farmers, and cultivated cassava, sweet potato, pumpkin, papaya, and pineapple. At sea, they fished for red snapper, kingfish and old wife. Along the shore they collected whelk, snails, lobster, conch, crab, and squid.

By the time Christopher Columbus arrived, the more war-like Caribe tribe had conquered the Arawak, and added yet another layer of culinary skill to the indigenous peoples.

Columbus, of course, arrived in the Virgins on a world-shaking quest for exotic foodstuffs. Back then, an ounce of black pepper was equal in worth to an ounce of pure gold.

The explorers immediately began searching ashore for cinnamon, cloves, nutmeg and pepper. Instead they discovered allspice, red pepper, and vanilla.

They also discovered the local produce. When they finally returned to the Old World, Christopher Columbus brought back corn, squash, tomatoes, potatoes, pumpkin, and avocados. These foods gradually transformed the diets of all Europeans.

Columbus didn't just export food from the region, however. He also imported some. It is believed he brought various plants and seeds aboard his ship, including orange seeds and sugar cane. (Three hundred years later, Captain Bligh of the *Bounty* brought breadfruit to the Caribbean.)

On the heels of the Spanish explorers, came the Dutch, Portuguese, English, French and Danes. By the early 1700's, virtually every island in the Caribbean had been claimed by Europeans.

The Danes were the first Europeans to settle on St. Thomas. After unsuccessful attempts from 1665 to 1668 to establish a colony, they finally established the settlement of Charlotte Amalie in 1672. The construction of Fort Christian began almost immediately. The Danes primary impetus to establish a colony on St. Thomas was profit-related. They realized that the island's large, safe harbor would allow it to become an international trade center—which it rapidly did.

The first generation of St. Thomas colonists were explorers and adventurers. Then came the farmers, merchants, and plantation owners. As the economy of the islands began to expand, so did its water-borne commerce. This attracted a large number of buccaneers and pirates.

The Danes, like their European counterparts on other nearby islands, began to cultivate the land soon after their arrival. At first, they grew cotton and tobacco, then sugar cane.

The cultivation of sugar cane was extremely labor intensive. The Danes began to import slaves from West Africa to do the arduous field work. By the end of the 1600's, there were about 600 West African slaves on St. Thomas.

St. Croix was alternately under the flags of England, France, and Spain——but the Danes finally took possession of it in 1735. (Of all three islands, St. Croix has the most flat, viable farm land.)

By the 1760's, the African slave population in the Virgin Islands was almost 17,000.

The African influence certainly was——and clearly still is——the major factor in shaping the cuisine of the Caribbean.

A slave's daily food ration was often quite meager despite their being forced to work long hours at hard labor in the hot sun. For the most part, they existed on such staples as cornmeal, salted fish, and bacon. A few slave families were allowed to cultivate small plots of land on which they grew cassava, yam, and corn.

African women became quite adept at making something tasty from almost nothing. To their sparse rations of salted fish and odd bits of meat, they added a growing number of home-grown vegetables and wild herbs. They simmered these flavorful morsels all day long in coal-fueled cast iron cook-pots.

From this tradition——often borne of poverty, misery and pain——come our hearty island soups of today.

As the 1600's turned into the 1700's, some of the Africans were able to grow a sufficient amount of food to supplement their family's supply——and have a little something left over. These small food surpluses gave birth to the traditional open-air markets where the African women brought their produce to sell. While selling their wares at market, they often traded with their fellow vendors for other goods their families needed.

This open-air market tradition continues to the present day, especially at Charlotte Amalie's Market Square on Saturday mornings.

Large scale plantation agriculture began to decline in the 1800's. In 1854, the Africans were emancipated from the bonds of slavery.

The next wave of immigrants wading ashore in the VI were the Chinese and East Indians. They arrived as indentured servants to fill the labor void created by the freeing of the slaves. The Chinese added their stir-fries and sweet & sour dishes to the culinary melting pot. The East Indians contributed such ingredients as wheat, rice, mango, eggplant, ginger, cloves, nutmeg, and curry to local dishes.

In 1917, the United States purchased the Virgin Islands (or more properly, the Danish West Indies) from the Danes.

Today, of course, people of many different nationalities continue to come to the USVI, both as residents and tourists. Results of the 1990 census showed a total island population of nearly 90,000. Residents are from all parts of Europe, Asia, Africa, North and South America, and numerous other islands in the Caribbean.

Thus, the cuisine of the Virgins is truly a unique mix of all the diverse cultures and different cuisines of the world.

Of course, our restaurants reflect this. We have numerous small 'local' restaurants which feature fish, fungi, and kallaloo.

There are also a number of sophisticated, cosmopolitan restaurants whose chefs are graduates of such prestigious institutions as New York's Culinary Institute of America. We have numerous restaurants which specialize in French, Italian, Spanish, Greek, Middle Eastern, Puerto Rican, and Chinese dishes.

Of course, we also have some uniquely American fast-food spots: Wendy's, McDonald's, Pizza Hut, Taco Bell, and Kentucky Fried Chicken.

Our grocery stores offer a similar diversity. In addition to open air markets which sell locally grown produce, there are numerous small road-side stands which sell fresh fish, fruits, and vegetables. (Many of these vendors buy direct from the funky down-island cargo ships which tie up alongside the seawall in Charlotte Amalie harbor.)

A number of Mom-and-Pop grocery stores still manage to thrive in the shadow of such national grocery chains as Grand Union, Plaza Extra, and Pueblo.

Today it is as easy to find a Twinkie or a can of Campbell's Chicken Noodle soup as it is to find a papaya or a mango.

# BEVERAGES & APPETIZERS

### BEVERAGES:

1. Coconut Water

2. Coconut Milk and Cream

3. Pina Colada

4. Ginger Beer

5. Guavaberry Liqueur

6. Planter's Punch

7. Iced Lemon Grass Tea

8. Hot Soursop Tea

9. Fresh Passion Fruit Drink

10. Hibiscus Aide

### APPETIZERS:

1. Bang!

2. Prosciutto & Mango

3. Plantain Chips

4. Conch Fritters

5. Spanikopita

## COCONUT

The coconut palm ranks as one of the ten most useful trees in the world. It's fruit, the coconut, has many, many uses. One of them is a great tropical drink.

The coconut is encased in a green or brown husk. When the husk is removed, the actual nut varies in size between a baseball and volleyball. It has a dark brown, hard, fibrous shell. When a coconut is young and has a green husk, there is coconut "water" inside and the white flesh is soft and jelly-like.

As the coconut matures and it's outer husk turns brown, the amount of coconut water decreases and the white flesh becomes firm.

## COCONUT WATER

On our way home from work each day, we pass 'the Coconut Man'——as my three-year-old son, Rian, likes to call him. The 'Coconut Man' always has the trunk of his car filled with delicious green coconuts which he sells.

With a long-blade knife, he deftly slices off the top of the coconut and then plops a straw inside for his customers. There is always a little crowd around him, waiting to quench their thirst in the afternoon's heat. On more than one occasion, we too have gathered around 'the Coconut Man'.

To enjoy this nearly clear, slightly sweet drink——you first must select the right coconut. These are widely available from local stores, at the open-air markets, or even up a nearby palm tree.

If the coconut is still in its husk, look for one that is green. Or, if the nuts have had their husk's removed, hold it up to your ear to check for the swishing sound of liquid inside as you shake it.

## GETTING THE COCONUT WATER

After removing the outer husk (if needed), locate the 'eyes' which are the three black spots at one end of the coconut. With an ice pick or a screwdriver and hammer, pierce at least two of these eyes. (Note: one of the eyes will be much easier to pierce than the others. This is the one through which the seedling would have eventually germinated.)

Drain and strain the clear liquid into a glass or small pitcher. Coconut water can be served at room temperature or chilled. Refrigerate any leftover coconut water. An 8 ounce cup of coconut water contains: 53 calories, 0.5 grams fat, 0 milligrams cholesterol and 60 milligrams sodium.

When the husk of the coconut is green, the inner meat is the soft consistency of jelly. Many people enjoy eating this 'coconut jelly'. All you need is an open coconut and a spoon.

## CRACKING OPEN THE COCONUT

Select a coconut with a brown husk, or one with little liquid inside. Drain the water from the coconut, as above, and smell it. If it emits a rancid odor, throw the coconut away. Otherwise, it is suitable for making coconut milk and coconut cream.

To break open the coconut, tap the shell a few times with a hammer. Then, place it on a hard surface——a sturdy table or the floor——and give it a walloping hard blow. It should break into several pieces. With the blunt end kitchen knife, pry the white coconut flesh away from the shell. Discard the shell and keep the flesh.

## COCONUT MILK & COCONUT CREAM

Coconut milk and coconut cream is made from the hard meat of a mature coconut.

After all the coconut flesh has been removed from its shell, cut it into small pieces so that it will fit into a blender or food processor. For one coconut, add 2 cups of liquid. This liquid can be a combination of coconut water and warm tap water or all warm tap water. Blend or process at high speed until the coconut is liquified. You may need to stop the blender or processor intermittently to scrape down any chunks of coconut that stick to the side of the container. When finished, strain the liquified coconut through a fine mesh strainer or piece of cheesecloth into a pitcher. Discard the pulp. The resulting rich liquid is coconut milk. A one-cup serving provides: 614 calories, 61 grams fat, 0 milligrams cholesterol and 128 milligrams sodium.

To make an even richer beverage called coconut cream, set a portion of coconut milk aside in the refrigerator. After a few hours, the cream will rise to the top. Skim off the thick top cream and store it in a separate container. A one-cup serving of coconut cream provides: 768 calories, 72 grams fat, 0 milligrams cholesterol and 16 milligrams sodium.

## ISLAND'S BEST PINA COLADA

Canned, sweetened coconut cream can be used to make this delightful frozen, rum-spiked drink. However, using fresh coconut cream tastes much better.

**1 cup unsweetened pineapple juice (\*)**
**1/2 cup coconut cream**
**1/2 cup light Virgin Islands rum**
**2 teaspoons sugar**
**2 tablespoons fresh lime juice**
**Ice cubes**
**Pineapple spears, grated coconut,**
**    maraschino cherries - or garnish,**
**    as desired**

Place pineapple juice, coconut cream, rum, sugar and lime juice in a blender and process until creamy and smooth. Add ice and blend an additional 30 seconds. Pour into serving glasses - or a fresh coconut cup - and garnish with pineapple, coconut and cherries, as desired.

Makes 2 servings. Per serving (without garnish): 329 calories, 21 grams fat, 0 milligrams cholesterol and 42 milligrams sodium.

(*) If you want your Island's Best Pina Colada to be truly island fresh, make your own pineapple juice by sieving pineapple slices through a fine mesh strainer or cheesecloth, to equal one cup of juice.

## COCONUT CUPS

What could be more tropical than serving your Island's Best Pina Colada—or any other fruit-flavored beverage—right out of the coconut itself?

To make a coconut cup, saw off the upper one-third of an empty coconut. To make a stable base for it, cut the smaller piece in half again. Place the wider side of the base down on the table, and insert the cup on top.

## GINGER SPICE

Fresh ginger is a favorite spice of many West Indian chefs. It is also the number one ingredient in the non-alcoholic beverage, ginger beer.

When selecting fresh ginger root, look for pieces that are rock-hard and heavy for their size. The most flavorful pieces have a smooth surface, thin skin, and are light tan in color. The less fibrous the root is, the better. You can get an idea as to the ginger's fiber content by inspecting a newly broken knob for loose fibers peeking out.

There are two ways to store ginger. Most conventionally, you can wrap the root in a paper towel, place it inside a plastic bag, and refrigerate it. Change the paper towel every week or when it becomes moist, and the ginger root will stay fresh up to 3 weeks.

The second way to store ginger root is to plant it in some sandy soil in a small pot. Place the pot on a window ledge or other sunny location. In a few days, small green sprouts will appear. When you need ginger, dig it up, cut off what you need, then replant it.

Ginger root can be used in making sauces, curries, cakes——and to season bananas, tomatoes, squash, onion and sweet potatoes. Like garlic, rubbing fish with fresh cut ginger can take away the fishy smell.

However, if you are looking for a cool, refreshing drink that's easy to make, use your ginger root to make Ginger Beer. This recipe is served at the *Sweet Life Cafe* in Smith Bay, St. Thomas:

## GINGER BEER

**6 pieces ginger root**
**1/2 gallon water**
**1 teaspoon vanilla or almond essence**
**1 cup honey**

Wash and grate ginger. No need to peel ginger first. Place grated ginger in water. Allow to soak for about one hour. Strain ginger pieces from the liquid. Flavor with essence and sweeten with honey.

Makes 8, one-cup servings. Per serving: 167 calories, 0 grams fat, 0 milligrams cholesterol and 2 milligrams sodium.

## MERRY CHRISTMAS GUAVABERRY

"Good Morning, Good Morning, I've come for my guavaberry..." These are the words to a popular holiday song that Virgin Islanders sing to their friends and neighbors while visiting on Christmas morning. Viola Krigger remembers collecting guavaberries as a young girl in St. Croix. She would spread a blanket under a guavaberry tree, and her strong brothers would shake the tree. This would cause the tiny berries to drop onto the blanket where they could be easily collected.

When they had collected enough, older family members would make guavaberry liqueur and tarts.

Today, guavaberries are harder to find. Unless of course, you happen to have a friend with a guavaberry tree growing in their yard. (Unfortunately, these luscious berries are rarely exported overseas).

Guavaberries are small red or yellow fruits. They are approximately the size of cranberries. They usually ripen in late fall. This is why products made from them, like guavaberry liqueur, are associated with the Christmas holidays.

To make guavaberry liqueur, the berries are mixed with the Virgin Island's own Cruzan rum, spices, dried fruits, and a few other ingredients. Then, the mixture is allowed to stand and ripen.

One of the old-time secrets to making excellent guavaberry liqueur is to use a bit of last year's batch when making a fresh one.

## GUAVABERRY LIQUEUR

**1 pound red guavaberries**
**1 pound yellow guavaberries**
**1 pound brown sugar**
**2 bottles (750 milliliter size) rum**
**1 pound prunes**
**1 pound raisins**
**3 sticks vanilla beans**
**1 pound sorrel**
**1/2 pound ginger root**
**3 sticks cinnamon bark**

Rinse berries with a small amount of water. Clean by popping berries and removing seeds. Rinse seeds, strain, and save liquid. (Be careful - guavaberries can leave a permanent stain on clothes!) Put seedless berries into a large pot, but reserve 1/2-cup yellow and 1/2-cup red berries for later use. Add liquid saved from rinsing seeds into the pot and add brown sugar.

Boil mixture until berries are soft. The juice should be a medium syrup consistency or sticky when cool. Mash or grind berries that were saved and mix with strongest, oldest rum available. To the cooled mixture, add prunes, raisins, vanilla beans, sorrel, ginger root and cinnamon bark. Pour into bottles or jars, cork, and wire down securely. Store in a dark place or cellar for several months. When guavaberry liqueur is fully ripened (the taste will tell), strain and re-bottle for later use.

Makes 24, 4 ounce servings. Per serving: 170 calories, 0 grams fat, 0 milligrams cholesterol and 53 milligrams sodium.

## VIRGIN ISLANDS RUM

Rum is the unofficial spirit of the West Indies. However it was in the *East* Indies, around 800 BC, that this intoxicating beverage was first produced. It took over 2000 years to reach Caribbean shores.

Columbus introduced sugar cane to the Virgin Islands on his second voyage in 1493. It was soon commercially grown in the Virgins on small plots. Over the course of the next 300 years, European immigrants set up vast sugar plantations on all three islands, and the Virgins became a major supplier of sugar to the Old World.

Of course, sugar cane was not valued solely for sugar. One of its major by-products is rum.

Rum is a complex spirit and can be described as the alcoholic distillation of the fermented juices of sugar cane, corn syrup or cane molasses, distilled at less than 190 proof. The Virgin Islands, in particular St. Croix, is a major rum producer. Local rums are sold under the labels of *Cruzan, Old St. Croix*, and *Brugal.*

Today, there are still public tours of the Cruzan Rum Pavilion on St. Croix. The island of St. Croix also offers a peek at a beautifully restored 18th century plantation at the Estate Whim Plantation Museum.

Sugar cane was king until the late 18th century when a Prussian chemist discovered how to extract sugar crystals from beets.

But even at its zenith, growing sugar was a difficult, time-consuming, financially risky task. It was also very labor-intensive. Local planters believed that sugar cane production was only profitable if the field workers were slaves. It was gruesome, dangerous, difficult work. During harvest, the slaves worked all day under the hot sun in the open fields, and then spent most of the night in the boiling rooms.

Planter's Punch, so the story goes, was what the planters drank after a long hot day of overseeing their estate's operations.

## PLANTER'S TROPICAL FRUIT PUNCH

**4 ounces Virgin Island rum**
**3 tablespoons water**
**4 tablespoons simple syrup (\*)**
**2 tablespoons fresh lime juice**
**Banana, mango, papaya, pineapple -**
    **cut into small chunks**
**Dash Angostura bitters**
**Crushed ice**
**Grated nutmeg**

Combine rum, water, simple syrup, lime juice, fruits and bitters. Pour into a tall glass and fill with ice. Sprinkle with grated nutmeg.

(\*) To make a simple syrup, combine 1/2 cup water and 1/2 cup granulated sugar in a saucepan. Bring to a rolling boil. Turn heat down and simmer for 1 to 2 minutes. Cool. Store in the refrigerator for use in making Planter's Tropical Fruit Punch. Makes 2 servings. Per serving: 91 calories, 0 grams fat, 0 milligrams cholesterol and 38 milligrams sodium.

## "BUSH" TEA IS OUR LOCAL "HERB" TEA

"Bush tea has traditionally been a part of our daily routine," said Virgin Islands agronomist Jacquel Dawson. "It was the food our grandparents gave us to sustain us. We drank it the first thing in the morning and the last thing at night."

Dawson has launched an agricultural business whose ambitious 'Project Bush Tea' will soon, he hopes, make the

Virgin Islands the 'Bush Tea Capitol of the Caribbean.'
What is bush tea? Bush is the term for local herbs. Therefore, bush teas are herb teas, made from some of the island's most fragrant, aromatic and delicious greenery. There are some 420 plants which have been used to make tea in the Virgin Islands. Some of these varieties have names similar to the trees on which they are found: sugar apple, mango, tamarind, sorrel, mint, and lime bush. Others have more interesting names: balsam, Japana, Spanish needle, worm grass, worry vine, jumbie pepper bush, pap bush, pasture fiddle, physic nut, bull tongue, chiggernut, belly ache bush, and inflammation bush. Some of these names give the clue that bush teas have customarily been used not only as thirst-quenching beverages, but also medicinally.

The most popular bush tea in the Virgin Islands is brewed from locally cultivated lemon grass. Lemon grass is a grass-like plant, like it's names implies, that has a delicate lemon smell and delicious lemon flavor. Traditionally, it was believed that a cup of Hot Lemon Grass Tea would help ease the discomfort of fevers and simple colds. It is also a refreshing drink, as anyone who has ever tasted it on a hot day will attest.

The leaves from the soursop tree also make a popular bush tea. The flavor of Hot Soursop Tea resembles the taste of the soursop's fruit (See page 158 for a description of the soursop fruit and a delicious Soursop Ice Cream recipe). Like lemon grass, soursop tea is believed to have a cooling effect on fevers.

# ICED LEMON GRASS TEA

**2 quarts water**
**1/2 bunch fresh lemon grass leaves**
**Sweetener of choice**

Boil leaves in water for 10 minutes. Remove tea leaves. Refrigerate tea for at least 2 hours. Pour over ice. For a distinctively different flavor, use honey instead of sugar for sweetener. It is best to add honey while the tea is hot, since it will mix better.

Makes 8 cups tea. Per serving (made with 1/2 cup sugar per recipe): 16 calories, 0 grams fat, 0 milligrams cholesterol and 0 milligrams sodium. Per serving (made with 1/2 cup of honey per recipe): 15 calories, 0 grams fat, 0 milligrams cholesterol and 0 milligrams sodium.

## HOT SOURSOP TEA

**1 cup boiling water**
**1 tea ball full of dried soursop leaves**
**Sweetener of choice**
**Slice of fresh lemon or lime (optional)**

Allow tea to steep for 3 to 5 minutes. Add honey or sugar to taste.

For a different flavor, add a slice of lemon or lime to the hot tea.

Makes 1 cup tea. Per serving (with 1 teaspoon honey): 15 calories, 0 grams fat, 0 milligrams cholesterol and 0 milligrams sodium. Per serving (with 1 teaspoon sugar): 16 calories, 0 grams fat, 0 milligrams cholesterol and 0 milligrams sodium.

## LOCAL FARMING

"Not only are the Virgin Islands able to produce food, but we are able to produce *high quality food*—food which is plump, sweet and nutritious," says full-time farmer Eldridge Thomas.

Thomas and his fellow farmers grow an amazing variety of fresh fruits and vegetables on the cool mountain slopes of St. Thomas' West End. They grow collard greens, scallions, kidney beans, squash, okra, eggplant, avocado, banana, soursop, cocoplums, cashew, guava, mango and mamey apple—to name but a few. There are nearly 100 full-time farmers in the three Virgin Islands. In addition to produce, Thomas is also a beekeeper. His bees perform double duty. They not only produce a deliciously sweet honey, but also pollinating his fruit trees.

Whenever there is a local food fair, Thomas makes one of his specialty fruit drinks, like Passion Fruit Drink.

## A LITTLE ABOUT THE PASSION FRUIT

Passion fruit are small, oval or egg-shaped fruit, which range in size from 1-1/2 to 2 inches in diameter. In the Caribbean, the passion fruit's hard thick skin is yellow in color. However, in other areas of the world, it may be purple or reddish gold. This aromatic, exotic tasting fruit's inner pulp is yellow-orange, has a gelatin like consistency and is spiked with numerous small black seeds.

The passion fruit received its distinguished name from Christian missionaries in South America during the 16th century. They saw the crown of thorns and the symbol of the crucifixion in the fruit's elegant flower.

Nutritionally, passion fruit are low in calories—having only 18 calories per fruit. It is a good source of Vitamin's A and C, and has a fair source of fiber. Like most fruit, passion fruit contain no significant fat, cholesterol, or sodium. It is also exported to the United States.

In the Virgin Islands, locally grown passion fruit are in season from spring to summer. When purchasing passion fruit, look for a smooth skin that has just begun to wrinkle. Prepare Thomas' Passion Fruit Drink as follows:

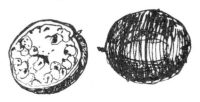

## FRESH PASSION FRUIT DRINK

**2 cups passion fruit pulp (18 to 20 passion fruits)**
**1 quart plus 8 ounces boiling water**
**1/2 cup sugar, or to taste**
**1 teaspoon vanilla essence**
**1 teaspoon almond essence**
**juice from 1 fresh lime**

Peel passion fruit. Place pulp in a large bowl. Add one quart boiling water and cover the pot. Let pulp in water sit at room temperature for 4 to 5 hours.

Strain the seeds through a colander. To get as much pulp from the seeds as possible, add 4 ounces boiling water to seeds while stirring.

Repeat rinsing the seeds with 4 ounces of boiling water once more.

Add sugar and adjust sweetness to taste. Add vanilla and almond essence and lime juice.

Refrigerate, then enjoy.

Makes 6 servings. Per serving: 112 calories, 0 grams fat, 8 milligrams cholesterol and 8 milligrams sodium.

### HIBISCUS

The red hibiscus flower, which is also known as the 'Rose of China', blooms almost everywhere in the Virgin Islands. This large, beautiful, brightly-colored, flower makes a tasty crimson-colored drink. Because the syrupy nature of this beverage, it has historically been used as a cough remedy.

Here is a recipe from Blanche Mills, of the University of the Virgin Islands Cooperative Extension Service.

# HIBISCUS AIDE

**15 individual red hibiscus blossoms**
**1 small knob fresh ginger (approx. 1/4 oz.)**
**6 cups water**
**Juice from 3 fresh limes**
**3/4 cup sugar, or to taste**
**Fresh limes, cut in slices for garnish**

Wash blossoms and ginger. Grate ginger and place it in a large saucepan. Cover with 2 cups of water and boil for 2 to 3 minutes. Add hibiscus blossoms. Remove pan from heat and cover.

When cool, strain liquid into a large pitcher. Add 4 cups of water and juice from limes. Add sugar to taste. Chill and serve cold over cracked ice. Garnish with fresh lime wedge, if desired.

Makes 6 servings. Per serving (made with 3/4 cup of sugar per recipe): 96 calories, 0 grams fat, 0 milligrams cholesterol and 3 milligrams sodium.

## CRUISING FARE

The waters of the Virgin Islands have more charterboats per square mile than anywhere else in the world. Thus, many of our finest chefs are sea-going ones. Despite the fact that they are usually forced to work out of a tiny kitchen (galley) about the size of a small closet, many charter chefs are able to turn out an amazing variety of gourmet food under the most adverse of culinary conditions.

Of course, appetizers play a large role in such a chef's life.

BANG! is a quick, delicious, easy-to-prepare snack or appetizer. It was created by charter chef Diana Horn of *Rangga*.

Ms. Horn's recipe is just one of the many recipes which local publisher Jan Robinson has gathered together in her cookbook, *Ship to Shore*.

## BANG!

**1 block Edam cheese, peeled**
**1 to 2 cloves garlic, minced**
**Sherry**
**10 refrigerated biscuits**

Preheat oven to 350 degrees. In a 9 inch glass pie dish, sprinkle minced garlic over bottom. Add enough sherry to cover bottom. Place peeled Edam in center. Surround with biscuits. Bake for 15 to 20 minutes or until biscuits are golden and the cheese is melted. Serve as is. Let the guests pull apart and spread melted cheese on hot biscuits.

Makes 10 appetizer servings. Per serving: 195 calories, 11 grams fat, 22 milligrams cholesterol and 443 milligrams sodium.

### MANGO MADNESS!

Salty, thin slices of prosciutto wrapped around honeydew melon wedges is a popular Italian appetizer. To give this dish a tropical flare, substitute the honeydew with soft, juicy slices of mango.

Mangoes are kidney-shaped fruit that turn from green to light yellow, orange and pink when ripe. In the Virgin Islands, mangoes are as popular as apples are on the U.S. mainland.

There are some 25 varieties of mangoes. They have names like marble, kidney, Tommy Adkins, big breed, and Julie. Each is slightly different in taste, but, in general, mangoes have a peach-like flavor.

Mangoes are the ultimate in clingstone fruits. It is very difficult to separate the fruit from the seed. Here are two methods for slicing a mango, which is the first step in preparing Prosciutto & Mango appetizer.

Method One

Begin by standing the mango upright on a cutting board. Cut vertically through the mango at a location about 1/4-inch from the center. This should enable you to slice off an oval of fruit while avoiding the center stone. Repeat this cut on the opposite side of the mango. Cut each half into three slices, lengthwise. Pare away mango skin on each slice as you would an apple.

Method Two

Holding the mango in the palm of your hand, make 4 to 6 scoring cuts (depending on the size of the fruit) in the skin. With the tip of the knife, lift a portion of skin by the stem and peel it back, removing it from the flesh. Repeat this process until the mango is completely peeled.

At this point, you can cut the mango into two pieces, one slightly bigger than the other (to avoid the stone). If desired, you can then cut those pieces into thirds. Or, you can make slices into the mango down to the stone and pull the individual slices free.

## PROSCIUTTO & MANGO

**Ripe mango, peeled and cut into 12 thin wedges**
**12 paper thin slices of prosciutto**

Wrap mango slices with prosciutto. Serve chilled.
Makes 6 appetizer servings: 74 calories, 3 grams fat, 16 milligrams cholesterol and 374 milligrams sodium.

## TROPICAL SNACKS

Looking for a tropical alterative to potato chips? Try plantain chips. Plantains resemble bananas, but are longer, thicker and starchier in flavor. They are used more like a vegetable, then a fruit. (See pages 67 for more recipes using plantains, and tips on how to peel this sometimes difficult food.) In many locations, plantain chips are sold in bags, but the homemade variety tastes much better. At an informal gathering of friends or prelude to a festive dinner party, plantain chips will be a tropical hit.

## PLANTAIN CHIPS

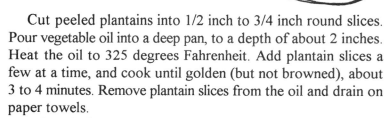

**3 large ripe plantains, peeled**
**Vegetable oil, for deep-fat frying**
**Salt, to taste**

Cut peeled plantains into 1/2 inch to 3/4 inch round slices. Pour vegetable oil into a deep pan, to a depth of about 2 inches. Heat the oil to 325 degrees Fahrenheit. Add plantain slices a few at a time, and cook until golden (but not browned), about 3 to 4 minutes. Remove plantain slices from the oil and drain on paper towels.

When drained, move plantain slices to a flat surfaced area, like a large cutting board or kitchen counter. Make sure to leave an inch of room between each slice. Using a meat mallet, pound each plantain slice to the thickness of a quarter.

Fill a pot with a quart of cold water. Add a teaspoon of salt to the water and stir to dissolve. Place pounded plantain slices into the salty water. Keep slices in the water for 2 to 3 minutes or until the edges of the slices absorb water and look puffy. Lift plantain slices out of water and drain on a fresh layer of paper towels.

Reheat vegetable oil to 375 degrees. When plantain slices are dry, transfer them back into the hot oil and cook until brown, about 3 minutes. Drain once again on paper towels. Sprinkle with salt to taste. Store any leftover plantain chips in an air-tight container to prevent them from becoming soggy in humid weather.

Makes 6 servings. Per serving (with 1/2 teaspoon salt sprinkled over recipe): 149 calories, 5 grams fat, 0 milligrams cholesterol and 195 milligrams sodium.

As a variation, flavor plantain chips with seasoned salt or cayenne pepper, or sprinkle with Parmesan cheese or serve with a hot and spicy salsa.

## SPRAT HALL'S FAMOUS FRITTERS

On the island of St. Croix at the *Sprat Hall Beach Restaurant,* James Herd has been cooking conch for over 30 years. "Back in the 1950's, I would go fishing or diving for conch and lobster," he said. "What I caught that day would be on the menu that night. Back then, there were lots of conch."

Herd prepares conch in a number of ways. For an appetizer, he sautes thin slices of conch and serves them with wild (sugarless) orange juice and horseradish. He makes conch 'creole-style' by grinding conch meat like hamburger, and then combining it with tomato, onion, celery, pepper and garlic. "Garlic helps bring out the flavor of conch," said Herd.

Conch chowder is another of the restaurant's menu items. It is made like New England clam chowder, with milk or cream and diced potatoes. Some customers like to add a dash of sherry.

Herd has his own style of conch salad which he serves either as a salad platter or as a sandwich filling. Finally, he also serves spicy hot Conch Fritters.

For tips on tenderizing conch and a Cold Conch Salad recipe from chef Alfredo Jeffers, see page 49.

# CONCH FRITTERS

**2 cups flour**
**1 tablespoon baking powder**
**Pinch salt**
**1 tablespoon garlic powder**
**1/2 cup evaporated milk or conch broth**
**2 cups ground conch meat**
**Red pepper, if desired**
**Vegetable oil, for deep-fat frying**

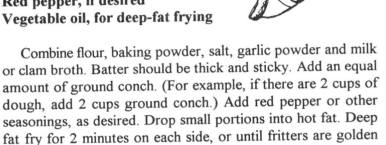

Combine flour, baking powder, salt, garlic powder and milk or clam broth. Batter should be thick and sticky. Add an equal amount of ground conch. (For example, if there are 2 cups of dough, add 2 cups ground conch.) Add red pepper or other seasonings, as desired. Drop small portions into hot fat. Deep fat fry for 2 minutes on each side, or until fritters are golden brown.

Makes 18 fritters. Per fritter: 118 calories, 5 grams fat, 12 milligrams cholesterol and 70 milligrams sodium.

## GREEK CUISINE IN A WEST INDIAN SETTING

Jim Boukas, Chef/Owner of *Zorba's*, offers authentic Greek cuisine in the heart of downtown Charlotte Amalie. "Olive oil, garlic, lemon, oregano, lamb, tomatoes, feta cheese and eggplant are some of the ingredients that are most popular in Greek dishes," said Boukas.

His menu is wonderfully varied. Melitzanosalata is an eggplant salad. Tzatziki are cucumbers in yogurt. (Boukas makes fresh bread and yogurt daily.) Moussaka is a popular lamb and eggplant casserole flavored with tomatoes. There is also a roast leg of lamb (seasoned with olive oil and garlic) which is grilled Greek style on a rotisserie.

Pizza, traditionally a food thought to be Italian in origin, is served at *Zorba's* with a distinctly Greek flair. A particularly delicious example comes with fresh tomatoes, oregano, and feta cheese.

One of the most important aspects of any pizza is its crust. Boukas's crusts are flavored in a mesquite burning oven. "This used to be the old 1854 house, one of the oldest single family dwellings in Charlotte Amalie," Boukas said, who rebuilt the old Danish oven within.

*Zorba's* open-air, flower-filled dining room is located in the residence's former courtyard. A gently trickling waterfall adds to the ambiance of the restaurant. "It reminds me of Greece," Boukas said.

The restaurant is in good company. On Government Hill where it is located, there is the delightful *Hotel 1829* and the Governor's official residence.

Here is Boukas' recipe for Spanikopita. This spinach and feta filled pastry makes a great start to any meal.

## *ZORBA'S* CLASSIC SPANIKOPITA

**prepared Phyllo dough**
**1-1/2 pounds fresh spinach**
**1/4 cup plus 3 tablespoons virgin olive oil**
**1/2 pound scallions, finely chopped**
**1 large leek, coarsely chopped**
**2 bunches fresh dill, chopped (can substitute fennel)**
**1 large bunch fresh parsley, chopped**
**1 egg, slightly beaten**
**3/4 pound feta cheese**
**2 tablespoons Greek or Parmesan cheese, grated**
**3/4 tablespoon nutmeg**
**1/2 teaspoon ground cumin**
**Salt and freshly ground pepper, to taste**
**1 egg yolk**
**2 tablespoons milk**

Remove Phyllo dough from refrigerator. Preheat oven to 375 degrees. Wash and chop spinach, squeeze dry and drain well. Heat 2 tablespoons olive oil in a heavy pan. Saute scallions and leek 5 to 7 minutes over medium heat until green part of leek is softened and scallions are almost translucent. Add spinach and stir until wilted. Remove mixture and let drain completely in a colander. Set aside and cool.

In a large bowl, combine cooled mixture, dill, parsley and add slightly beaten egg, 1/4 cup olive oil, feta, Parmesan cheese, spices, salt and pepper. Mix thoroughly with a wooden spoon.

Divide Phyllo dough in half. On a lightly floured surface, roll out first half to a circle of about 12 inches. Place in a lightly oiled pie pan. Brush with remaining tablespoon of olive oil. Spread spinach filling evenly over dough.

Roll out remaining dough to a 12 inch circle and place over top of filling. Press edges together and cut away extra dough, leaving about 1/2 inch to roll toward inner rim of pie pan.

Make 4 small incisions in center of pie. Brush top with egg yolk and milk mixture. Bake 40 minutes or until crust is golden brown.

Serve warm or cold.

Makes 12 servings. Per serving: 267 calories, 19 grams fat, 66 milligrams cholesterol and 607 milligrams sodium.

# SALADS

1. Avocado Filled With Saltfish Salad

2. Spicy Scallops on Mixed Greens

3. Fruit Salad with Aloe

4. Sea Purslane Egg Salad

5. Cold Conch Salad

6. Steak & Potato Salad

7. Spring Lobster & Asparagus Salad

8. Po-Pa Salad

9. Wilted Spinach Salad

## SALTFISH

Saltfish in the islands is nearly synonymous with salted cod. It's popularity is a carry-over from 'the days of old' when there was no refrigeration. Drying and salting were good methods of food preservation, even in the tropics. Saltfish's popularity makes it a prime ingredient in many West Indian recipes.

To convert the hard block of salted cod you purchase in the grocery into an edible ingredient, follow these steps:

1. Use a sharp knife or cleaver to cut the large piece of salted cod into smaller chunks that will fit into either a saucepan or soup kettle, depending on the quantity.

2. Fill saucepan or kettle with cold water, then place on top of the stove and heat until boiling.

3. After salted cod has come to a boil, turn off heat and allow to cool for at least 8 to 12 hours or overnight.

4. Drain water from salted cod and remove bones and skin, if necessary.

5. Shred fish with a fork, then fill saucepan or kettle once again with water and heat until boiling.

6. Cool salted cod and drain well in a colander or sieve.

7. If the fish still tastes too salty, boil, cool and drain once again.

When time is too short for an overnight soak, you can try this quicker method:

1. Place cut chunks of salted cod in a saucepan or kettle, cover with water and bring to a boil.

2. Continue boiling salt cod until it has reached the desired flavor of saltiness. Frequent taste tests along the way will assist in this process.

Once cod is desalted, by either method, flake it with a fork. It is now ready for use. As a rule of thumb, one pound of dry salted cod will yield about two cups cooked, flaked fish. Desalted codfish differs from fresh in that it has a texture and flavor all its own. For this reason, substituting fresh codfish for the salted variety will just not be the same.

## AVOCADO FILLED WITH SALTFISH SALAD

1 pound salted codfish
2 fresh tomatoes, chopped
4 scallions, sliced thin
1 green pepper, seeded and diced
Dash Tabasco
1/2 cup vegetable oil
2 tablespoon fresh lemon or lime juice
2 avocados, cut in half with pits removed
Lettuce leaves (iceberg, romaine, bibb
    or a combination of the three are nice)
2 hard-cooked eggs, sliced in wedges or circles

Soak salted cod to remove excess salt. Place flaked codfish in a large mixing bowl and combine with tomatoes, scallion, green pepper and Tabasco. Mix together oil and lemon or lime juice, then pour over codfish mixture. Toss gently. Spoon saltfish salad into avocado halves. Line individual serving plates with lettuce and place filled avocado halves on top. Garnish

with hard-cooked eggs.
    Makes 4 servings. Per serving: 584 calories, 46 grams fat, 156 milligrams cholesterol and 419 milligrams sodium. (Note: sodium values for salt cod recipes can vary greatly according to how thoroughly the saltfish is soaked).

## A COOL SALAD FOR A HOT DAY

    The ever-blowing tradewinds usually keep the Virgin Islands relatively cool. But some days, especially in the summer months, it can be rather warm. Sarah Bowman, executive chef at the *Stouffer Grand Beach Resort*, reports that many of her guests have been requesting lighter fare lately. She believes that these requests have been prompted both by the growing national trend towards healthier eating and an effort to beat the tropical heat.
    One of Bowman's most popular answers to her guest's requests has been her Spicy Scallop Mixed Greens with Cucumber & Dill Dressing. Her trick for lowering calories and keeping the salad light is to replace a portion of the sour cream in the dressing with low-fat yogurt. The taste is spectacular!

## SPICY SCALLOP SALAD

**12 jumbo scallops**
**Cajun seasoning**
**1 fresh cucumber**
**1/8 bunch fresh dill**
**1/4 cup low-fat yogurt**
**1/4 cup sour cream**
**1/2 small onion**
**Mixed greens**

    Roll scallops in Cajun seasoning, then grill. Peel and remove seeds from cucumber. Combine half the cucumber, dill, yogurt, sour cream and onion in a blender and puree until smooth. To assemble, on each salad plate, place four long thin slices of cucumber to form a square. Place tossed greens in the center. Toss grilled scallops in dressing and then place on top of greens. Makes 4 servings. Per serving: 131 calories, 4 grams fat, 35 milligrams cholesterol and 158 milligrams sodium.

## LIVING OFF THE LAND - JADAN-STYLE

Have you ever tried eating the crispy blossoms of an aloe plant? Or, how about the succulent leaves of the little green plant called sea purslane (which grows alongside tropical shorelines like a fine green carpet). These are just two of the novel local ingredients used by Ivan and Doris Jadan in some of their favorite recipes.

The warm sun, blue sky, and green hills of St. John immediately captivated Ivan Jadan when he first visited the Virgin Islands in 1955. He knew of no other place which would make for a better home for him and his wife Doris.

Of course, life was different on St. John forty years ago. The population was less than 800 back then. The ferry service to St. Thomas was limited to twice per week. There were no well-stocked grocery stores or markets on the island.

So Ivan and Doris began to explore ways of living off the land.

As a boy, Ivan learned how to cook by watching his Ukrainian aunt while she prepared meals for the family. Ivan taught Doris the basic cooking techniques, and she soon applied these to local fruits, vegetables, and seafood. Their experimentation led to some highly unusual, and quite tasty discoveries.

The Jadans gathered their recipes together and produced *The Virgin Islands Cook House Cookbook*. In 1969, Doris, a teacher by profession, developed the Environmental Studies Program for our local schools. In this program, she taught school children about the living world around them. *VI Cuisine* with Ivan and Christine, was their second book. It used traditional foods in recipes featuring less sugar, salt, and fat.

Interestingly, Ivan's Russian influence has made these the only West Indian & Ukrainian cookbooks to ever be written. (The sale of the Jadans' cookbooks have been used to fund college scholarships for St. John youth.)

How did aloe blooms become incorporated into an Aloes Easter Fruit Salad? Doris explained that after a long winter dry spell, aloe is one of the first plants to bloom, usually by Easter.

Aloe blossoms are green-yellow. They appear on a central three-prong stalk that can grow up to eighteen inches high. As many as 20 blooms can be found on a single plant. Doris found that unopened aloe blossoms added color, texture, and flavor when sprinkled on top of a fruit salad.

Sea purslane has only 21 calories per cup, but is a rich source of iron, potassium, oxalate, and Vitamin C. It also contains a fair amount of naturally occurring sodium. Ivan and Doris have found chopped sea purslane leaves an excellent flavor enhancer for their Sea Purslane Egg Salad.

Ever heard of Cactus Soup? On page 93 is Jadan's recipe for this unique dish.

## ALOES EASTER FRUIT SALAD

**2 bananas, sliced in 1/4-inch circles**
**3 tart apples, (peeled or unpeeled) and diced**
**1/3 cup mayonnaise**
**1/4 cup diced celery**
**1/4 cup chopped almonds or pecans**
**Lettuce leaves**
**1/4 cup aloe blossoms**

Combine all ingredients together and mix well. Serve on a bed of lettuce leaves. Sprinkle aloe blossoms across the top of the salad.

Makes 6 servings. Per serving: 207 calories, 13 grams fat, 7 milligrams cholesterol and 83 milligrams sodium.

## SEA PURSLANE EGG SALAD

**6 hard boiled eggs, shelled and chopped**
**2 sweet pickles, chopped**
**3 green onions, chopped**
**1/2 cup sea purslane leaves, chopped**
**1/2 cup celery, chopped**
**1/3 cup mayonnaise**

Combine all ingredients well. Makes 6 servings: 174 calories, 15 grams fat, 220 milligrams cholesterol and 254 milligrams sodium.

## A TOUGH CONCH CAN BE A TENDER TREAT

The Queen Conch (Strombus gigas) is a marine creature prized both for its beautiful shell and its sweet meat. While conch is truly one of the island's seafood delicacies, if it is not carefully prepared it can be tough and tasteless. Here is a good way, although a bit time consuming, to prepare conch for this delicious salad.

1. Either remove the conch meat from the shell or from the wrapper after purchasing it at the grocery.(Check old conch shells to find where to break shell and cut attaching muscle of the conch.)

2. Lay the uncooked meat on a large board. With a mallet or a hammer, pound the conch, taking care to pound every portion of the flesh, for about 5 minutes. Well-pounded conch will have flattened out considerably and have no hard

thick lumps remaining visible. Fresh conch meat can be frozen prior to or after pounding. Freezing will also help to tenderize the flesh.

4. After pounding the conch, cut the meat into small strips and pressure cook it. Chef Alfredo Jeffers, who works at Iggie's at the Limetree Beach Resort, recommends a pressure cooking time of about 2 hours, in order for the conch to be well tenderized. Adding fresh lemon or lime juice to the cooking water will help the tenderizing process.

After it has been tenderized, the conch is ready to be included into dishes like Jeffers' Cold Conch Salad. There are many other dishes that can be made with conch. Look on page 40 for James Herd's recipe for spicy hot Conch Fritters.

## COLD CONCH SALAD

**1 pound cleaned conch, cooked and diced**
**1 medium tomato, diced**
**1 medium cucumber, peeled and diced**
**1/2 red onion, finely chopped**
**juice of 2 fresh limes**
**Juice of 1/2 fresh orange**
**1/2 teaspoon ground black pepper**
**1 teaspoon salt**
**1/2 red hot pepper, diced (\*)**
**1 green pepper, diced**
**1 clove garlic, minced**
**Romaine or Leaf lettuce leaves**

Combine all ingredients in a large mixing bowl, preferably while the conch is warm, and mix well. Refrigerate salad for at least an hour. Serve chilled.

Makes 6 servings. Per serving: 144 calories, 0 grams fat, 61 milligrams cholesterol and 465 milligrams sodium. (*) When handling chili peppers, either wear plastic kitchen gloves or wash hands well after touching peppers. Capsicum, the substance in chili peppers which makes them taste hot, can irritate the skin and eyes.

## LIGHT VERSIONS OF HEARTY FAVORITES

At *Marriott's Frenchman's Beach Resort's 'Tavern-on-the-Beach'*, chefs Wellman Smith and Cary Michael Neff have pleased both visitors and residents alike with their regional American cuisine. While they serve traditional favorites like roast turkey, Smithfield ham, and sirloin steaks—they often do so with a novel twist.

For example, Smith and Neff's Steak & Potato Salad combines a 12-ounce grilled sirloin steak, with grilled potato slices, grilled mushroom caps, and a fresh salad of mixed baby field greens. It's a light, fairly lean salad that eats like a hearty steak dinner.

# STEAK AND POTATO SALAD

12 ounce sirloin steak
Olive oil
Fresh rosemary
Fresh chopped garlic
3 fresh mushrooms
1 small potato

Salad Dressing:
2 cups milk
4 ounces bacon
1 onion, chopped
1/2 bunch fresh parsley
2 tbsp Dijon mustard
Red onion, chopped
1 cup heavy cream
1 tbsp garlic powder
3 tbsp Worcestershire sauce
5 cups mayonnaise
Salt and pepper
Blue cheese, crumbled
Mixture of fresh baby field greens & Plum tomatoes, sliced

Brush steak with olive oil, rosemary and garlic. Grill to desired stage of doneness. Slice steak thin, on the bias.

Cut stems from mushrooms. Wash potato well, then cut into quarters lengthwise. Brush mushrooms and potato slices with olive oil, place on grill and cook until done.

Fry bacon until crisp, then drain well. In a blender, combine bacon with onion, parsley, mustard, milk, cream, garlic powder, Worcestershire sauce, mayonnaise, salt and pepper, to taste. Blend until creamy.

To assemble plate, place baby field greens, sliced plum

tomatoes and chopped onion on one half of plate. Add mushroom caps to top of greens and sprinkle salad with crumbled blue cheese. Lay two potato quarters each on either side of salad. Place sliced beef on plate opposite salad. Serve dressing on the side.

Makes 1 salad. Per serving (excluding dressing and excluding salt to taste): 876 calories, 38 grams fat, 250 milligrams cholesterol and 203 milligrams sodium. Per tablespoon dressing: 70 calories, 6 grams fat, 8 milligrams cholesterol and 141 milligrams sodium.

## LOCAL LOBSTERS

Encased in its bright red segmented shell, a cooked lobster is truly a culinary delicacy. It only requires a little melted butter to make it the star attraction of any meal.

There are four main types of lobster——spiny or rock, clawed, slipper, and langostinos or squat. It is the spiny or rock lobster which is found in the Virgin Islands.

The most noticeable difference between the spiny or rock lobster and the variety most visitors are accustomed to eating is the absence of the giant front claws. The sweet meat of the body is comparable between the two.

Caribbean lobster is served many ways at the *Entre Nous* restaurant on St. Thomas, including this delicious Spring Lobster & Asparagus Salad:

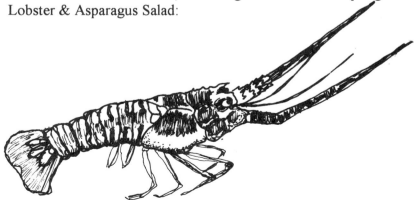

# SPRING LOBSTER & ASPARAGUS SALAD

**8 ounces fresh asparagus,**
  **cut into 2-inch pieces**
**6 ounces shredded green cabbage**
**1 to 1-1/2 pounds cooked lobster**
  **meat, cut into bite-sized pieces**
**3 tablespoons virgin olive oil**
**1 tablespoon tarragon vinegar**
**2 teaspoons chopped fresh tarragon**
**1/4 teaspoon salt**
**Pepper, to taste**
**Tarragon sprigs, for garnish**

Steam asparagus for 6 to 7 minutes until tender, yet crispy. Add cabbage and steam for an additional two minutes. Arrange asparagus, cabbage and lobster on four serving plates.

Make the dressing by mixing oil, vinegar, tarragon, salt and pepper in a screw-top jar. Shake well to combine. Sprinkle dressing over salads then garnish with sprigs of fresh tarragon.

Makes 4 servings: 189 calories, 11 grams fat, 61 milligrams cholesterol and 461 milligrams sodium.

## FOOD FAIRS

First there was 'Granny's Pot', then 'Man's Pot', and finally 'Food Melee.' These tasty gatherings——held on the rolling greens of University of the Virgin Islands golf course——offer residents a chance to sample a wide variety of exotic dishes while mingling with our local college professors.

"Our afternoon on the green is a wonderful opportunity for the entire community to come together. Our local cooks are the stars," explained organizer Geraldine Smith.

One of the participants who contributed a dish for the 'Food Melee' was Bernice A. Martin. Her delicious Po-Pa Salad offered a curious blend of both white potato and green papaya.

## CAN I EAT A GREEN PAPAYA?

In the Caribbean there are many examples of produce which can be eaten like a fruit when ripe, and like a vegetable when green. For example, ripe yellow bananas make sweet snacks, desserts, and beverages. Unripe green bananas are peeled, boiled, and served alongside fish as a starchy side dish. Green, unripe mangoes, are used to make a spicy chutney. At the orange-yellow ripe stage, they make marvelous sweet juice drinks, desserts, and snacks.

Likewise, green, unripe papaya can be peeled, steamed, and used in savory dishes, but it's the deep orange ripe ones which are best used in a sweet dish or beverage.

Papaya can grow large. They can weigh anywhere between one and ten pounds. They are low in calories, with only about 55 per cup. They are also good sources of Vitamins C and A, as well as potassium.

To make Po-Pa Salad, select a papaya before it begins to turn orange and soften.

# PO-PA SALAD

1 small or 1/2 large green
    papaya (about 1 pound)
3 eggs
1 cup mayonnaise
2 tablespoons vegetable oil
1/4 teaspoon salt
Black pepper
4 medium white potatoes,
    peeled and cubed
1 tablespoons prepared mustard
1/2 cup "seasoning" made
    from minced fresh:
    onion, green pepper, celery
    and thyme

Cut papaya in half lengthwise. Scoop out small black seeds lining the inner cavity. Peel away outer green skin. Cut papaya into cubes.

Place papaya in large pot, cover with water and bring to a boil. Add potatoes and salt. Cook papaya and potatoes 25 to 30 minutes or until tender. Remove papaya and potatoes from water, place in a large non-metal bowl and allow to cool.

Place eggs in a saucepan. Cover with water and cook until hard-boiled. Cool eggs in cold water after boiling. When cool, remove shells and chop.

When papaya and potatoes are cool, add shelled, chopped, hard-cooked eggs, mayonnaise, oil, mustard and seasonings. Mix well, adding black pepper and additional salt to taste. Chill and serve cold.

Makes 8 servings. Per serving: 391 calories, 29 grams fat, 102 milligrams cholesterol and 245 milligrams sodium.

## A SPECIAL SALAD

The *Hotel 1829* was built as a residence in (surprise!) 1829 by a prominent local sea captain. Today it houses one of St. Thomas' most renowned restaurants.

This restaurant——a favorite of former president Harry Truman and such contemporary stars as Paul McCartney, Tom Sellick, Robin Leach, and Dionne Warwick——is celebrated for its delightful atmosphere, wonderful service, and fine food.

One of their most popular salads is their Wilted Spinach Salad. It is created right in front of you. The chef wheels a cart——which contains a large bowl of fresh spinach greens, the dressing ingredients, and a sizzling hot saucepan——right over to your table.

The high alcohol content of the dressing makes it easy for the chef to set aflame. He quickly pours the flaming dressing over the greens, and then inverts the saucepan on top of the salad bowl. This holds in the heat, and wilts the greens.

While the splendid setting of *Hotel 1829* enhances any meal, their Wilted Spinach Salad loses nothing in the translation to your dinner table at home.

## WILTED SPINACH SALAD

**1 tablespoon butter**
**4 slices bacon**
**4 ounces olive oil**
**1 tablespoon chopped shallots**
**1 tablespoon chopped onions**
**1 teaspoon sugar**
**1 tablespoon red wine vinegar**
**Juice 1 lemon**
**Salt and pepper, to taste**
**1 ounce Cointreau**
**1 tablespoon Dijon mustard**
**1 ounce brandy**
**1-1/2 pounds fresh spinach**
**1/2 pound sliced mushrooms**
**1 tablespoon grated Parmesan cheese**
**Freshly ground black pepper, for garnish**

Preheat a 10 to 12-inch skillet over a medium flame. Add butter and bacon. Cook bacon until crisp.

Make dressing by combining olive oil, shallots, onions, vinegar, sugar, salt and pepper. Pour dressing into warm skillet along with Dijon mustard and lemon juice. Add brandy and Cointreau. Flame to remove most of the alcohol. Sauce will begin to look more like a salad dressing at this point.

On the side, make salad by combining spinach, mushrooms, onion and Parmesan cheese.

Take the skillet containing hot dressing and pour it over salad ingredients. Keep hot pan inverted over owl containing salad for one minute to wilt the greens. Take hot skillet off, toss salad and serve on individual plates. Garnish with freshly ground black pepper. Makes 6 servings. Per serving (with 1/2 teaspoon salt used for recipe): 246 calories, 23 grams fat, 9 milligrams cholesterol and 317 milligrams sodium.

## SIDE DISHES

**1. Coconut Red Beans & Rice**

**2. Black Beans & Rice**

**3. Garden Grilled Vegetables with Herb Vinaigrette**

**4. Grilled Zucchini & Eggplant Kabobs**

**5. Okra Fungi**

**6. Boiled Plantain**

**7. Mashed Plantain**

**8. Fried Ripe Plantain**

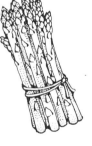

**9. Potato Stuffing**

**10. Penne Alla Caprese**

**11. Hercules' Docouna**

**12. Asparagus Pudding**

**13. Macaroni & Cheese**

## BEANS & RICE - A NATURAL COMBINATION

A few hundred years ago, the Spaniards introduced 'rice and beans' to the islands. This dish is still popular today. Rice and beans are not only tasty, but nutritious too. Their combined protein value is equal to fish, poultry, or red meat. Dried beans are rich in iron. Their high fiber content can help reduce blood cholesterol. Rice is often fortified with B-vitamins. Unfortunately, not all rice is the same. The white variety, which is the most popular, is lacking in the fiber content. Brown rice is much better for you.

Uncle Ben's long-grain rice seems the most preferred type by island residents. The terms 'beans' and 'peas' are often used interchangeably. The most common are red kidney beans, black beans, black-eyed peas, and pigeon peas. When selecting dried beans and peas consider the following:

Do the beans and peas have a bright, uniform color? Avoid those which are faded. A cloudiness on the surface may indicate mold.

Are the beans or peas all the same size? A mixture of different sizes will result in the smaller ones being overcooked while the larger ones remain hard.

Do the beans or peas have cracked skins, bits of dirt, dust or other unknown material in the bag or damage to the packaging itself? If so, look for better beans and peas elsewhere.

Although rice and bean dishes are tasty and nutritious, many people avoid them. Why? Gas. Here are three ways to remedy this common problem:

1. Keep the meal light. Don't eat these foods with a lot of fat

or in large quantities——especially if you are not accustomed to a high-fiber diet.

2. Time of day is important. Earlier is better than later because the digestive system works best when you are active. Eat beans and peas for lunch, for example, rather than at dinner.

3. Cook beans thoroughly to lessen their chance of producing gas. Sometimes adding garlic, cumin, ground coriander or a little vinegar near the end of cooking also helps.

Try these recipes for Coconut Red Beans & Rice and Black Beans & Rice:

## COCONUT RED BEANS & RICE

**1-1/2 cups dried red kidney beans**
**1 clove garlic, minced**
**4 cups water**
**Salt, to taste**
**1/2 fresh coconut**
**2 cups boiling water**
**Black pepper, to taste**
**2 green onions, chopped**
**1 teaspoon fresh thyme leaves**
**     (or 1/4 tsp dried)**
**1 fresh hot pepper**
**2 cups uncooked rice**

Combine beans, garlic, water and salt in a medium-sized saucepan. Cook covered, over moderate heat until beans are tender or about 2 hours.

Cut coconut meat into small pieces and place in a blender.

Blend as fine as possible. Pour boiling water over liquefied coconut and let stand for about 30 minutes. Run coconut milk through a fine mesh strainer to separate out coconut solids.

Add the coconut milk, black pepper, green onions, thyme and whole hot pepper to the cooked beans. Bring back to a boil, then remove the hot pepper. Add rice and stir. Return mixture to a boil, cover, reduce the heat and simmer for about 30 minutes or until all the liquid has been absorbed.

Makes 6 servings. Per serving: 332 calories, 5 grams fat, 0 milligrams cholesterol and 258 milligrams sodium.

## BLACK BEANS & RICE

**2 tablespoons olive oil**
**1 onion, finely chopped**
**1 clove garlic, minced**
**1 small green bell pepper, seeded and finely chopped**
**2 tomatoes, peeled, seeded and chopped**
**Salt and black pepper, to taste**
**2 cups cooked black beans**
**1 cup uncooked rice**
**2 cups cold water**

Heat the oil in a saucepan and add the onion, garlic and pepper. Saute until the onion is tender. Add the tomatoes and cook, stirring until the mixture is well blended and thick. Season to taste with salt and pepper. Stir in the black beans and mix well. Add rice and water, mixing lightly. Cover and cook over very low heat until rice is tender and water is absorbed.

Makes 6 servings. Per serving (with 1/2 teaspoon salt used for recipe): 246 calories, 5 grams fat, 0 milligrams cholesterol and 260 milligrams sodium.

## GREAT GRILLED VEGETABLES

St. Thomas' Magens Bay——named by National Geographic Magazine as one of the top 10 most beautiful beaches in the world——is a great place for a barbecue. Many local families gather here to grill steaks, chicken, and fish on a grill.

But meat and fish aren't the only thing you can grill. Vegetables are also tasty. We grill zucchini squash, corn, tomatoes, onions, red peppers, and eggplant as well.

Here are seven tips for grilling great vegetables, and two of our favorite recipes.

Begin with a clean grill because vegetables easily absorb flavors from other foods. You do not want last week's barbecued chicken to flavor tonight's vegetables.

Light the fire by using an electric starter or a cone-shaped cylinder. Do not use liquid starters. The delicate vegetables can pick up the residue.

Vegetables cook more quickly than meats, so watch them carefully. Do not cook vegetables over red hot coals. In just one minute, a slice of zucchini can be burnt outside but still raw inside. You may want to start with grilling just one variety of vegetable until you become comfortable. Take notes on the time it takes to cook each type of vegetable so you can coordinate them with other menu items in future meals.

If your grill is small and you do not have room for both meat and vegetables at once, grill the meat first and keep it warm. Clean the grill with a wire brush, then cook the vegetables.

When grilling meat, chicken or seafood together with vegetables on a skewer, cut the vegetables so that they will cook in the same amount of time as the other food. Also, choose vegetables that take the same length of time to cook as the meat, chicken or seafood. For example, choose green onions, mushrooms and cherry tomatoes when grilling quick-cooking shrimp or fish. Or, select green pepper, onion, squash or zucchini when grilling beef. To add long cooking vegetables to a quick cooking fish or shellfish, blanch them first to make up the difference in cooking time.

Whatever vegetable you use, always lightly coat it with oil so that it will cook evenly.

When grilling vegetables directly on the grill, cut them large enough so that they do not fall onto the coals. For example, cut zucchini lengthwise rather than crosswise.

Try these recipes for Garden Grilled Vegetables with Herb Vinaigrette and Grilled Zucchini & Eggplant Kabobs.

## GRILLED VEGETABLES

**4 ears of corn with husks**
**3 medium-sized zucchini squash**
**2 large red peppers, 2 large yellow peppers**
**1 pound large mushrooms**
**3/4 cup olive oil**
**1/3 cup red wine vinegar**
**1 tablespoon chopped fresh oregano (or 1 tsp dried)**
**1 tablespoon fresh thyme leaves (or 1 tsp dried)**
**1 teaspoon salt**
**1 teaspoon sugar**
**1/2 teaspoon freshly ground black pepper**

Carefully pull back husks half-way from each ear of corn and remove silk. Re-wrap corn with husk. Place corn with husks in a large pot and cover with cold water. Let them soak for 30 minutes to an hour. Soaking keeps corn moist and tender for grilling.

Cut zucchini and peppers in half lengthwise. Then, cut each half crosswise and discard the inner seeds. Trim tough ends from mushrooms.

In a large mixing bowl, make herb vinaigrette by combining olive oil, vinegar, oregano, thyme, salt, sugar and pepper. Add all vegetables to the dressing, except corn, and toss well to coat.

Remove corn from the water and shake off excess water. Place corn on center of the grill and arrange remaining vegetables on grill around corn. Reserve the dressing.

Cook vegetables over medium-low heat, turning vegetables occasionally. Cook corn about 45 minutes, red and yellow peppers about 30 minutes, zucchini about 20 minutes and mushrooms about 10 to 15 minutes.

Remove peppers, zucchini and mushrooms to a bowl with reserved dressing after they have finished cooking. Toss to coat. Remove corn from husks, cut into 2-inch chunks and toss with vegetables. Serve warm or refrigerate to serve cold later. Makes 4 servings. Per serving: 278 calories, 15 grams fat, 0 milligrams cholesterol and 286 milligrams sodium.

## GRILLED ZUCCHINI & EGGPLANT KABOBS

1 small eggplant, peeled if desired, cut into 1 inch chunks
2 small tomatoes, cut into quarters
1 medium-sized zucchini cut into 1 inch chunks
1 medium-sized yellow squash, cut into 1 inch chunks
4 tbsp olive oil
1/2 tsp freshly ground black pepper
1/4 tsp salt
2 tbsp red wine vinegar
1 large clove garlic, crushed
1-1/2 tsp chopped fresh mint leaves (or 1 tsp dried)

Begin fire in grill and place grill rack 5 to 6 inches from the coals. Alternate chunks of vegetables on 8 inch metal skewers, as desired. Brush vegetables with olive oil and sprinkle with salt and pepper. When coals are medium-hot, place kabobs on grill rack. Cook 10 to 12 minutes, turning three to four times until vegetables are browned and tender.

In a small mixing bowl and using a fork, beat two tablespoons oil, vinegar, garlic and mint to mix well. Brush this mixture over kabobs during the last two minutes of cooking. Remove kabobs to a warm platter and brush with any remaining garlic mixture.

Makes 4 servings. Per serving: 109 calories, 5 grams fat, 0 milligrams cholesterol and 143 milligrams sodium.

## FUNGI

Fish-and-fungi, like a hamburger-and-french-fries or chicken-and-rice, are two foods which are not the same without the other. A combination of the two makes for a perfect meal. Fish and fungi is so popular in the Virgin Islands that it could be called the unofficial national dish.

While most visitors to the island are familiar with a variety of fish dishes, fungi is unfamiliar. Fungi can be described simply as a stiff cornmeal mush. It is made from fine milled cornmeal. The trick is to stir the fungi properly so that it is velvety smooth, not lumpy. Fungi can be served plain or with the addition of chopped okra.

On an historic note, fish and fungi's roots lead back to the days of slavery. Danish Law allowed each slave six quarts of Indian meal and six salt herring per week. Occasionally, there were other foods thrown into the ration like yams. But the mainstay of cornmeal and fish led the African women to the creative result of fish and fungi.

Today, fungi is usually served with boiled local fish and topped with gravy.

# OKRA FUNGI

**10 ounce package frozen cut okra**
**2-1/2 cups boiling water**
**1-1/2 cups fine yellow cornmeal**
**2 tablespoons butter**
**1/4 teaspoon salt**
**Pepper, to taste**

Place frozen okra in boiling water. Cook until just barely tender.

In a medium size saucepan, bring 2-1/2 cups water to a boil. To make fungi that is free of lumps, mix about 1/4 cup of the cornmeal with 3/4 cup water in a separate small bowl. Then, add this mixture back into the larger pot of boiling water. Let cornmeal cook for about a minute. Then, add the rest of the cornmeal into the pan in a slow steady stream, while stirring constantly.

Add hot cooked okra to cooked cornmeal. Stir well. Stir in the butter, salt and pepper, to taste. Simmer for about 5 minutes more. Serve piping hot with Boiled Fish West Indian Style.

Makes 8 servings. Per serving: 132 calories, 3 grams fat, 7 milligrams cholesterol and 98 milligrams sodium.

## PLANTAINS

The banana-looking plantain is served as a starchy vegetable—boiled, mashed, or fried—with meat, poultry, and fish dishes in many Caribbean meals.

Plantains are unripe when their skin is green, and ripe when their skin is yellow with black spots. Properly cooked, they are tasty both ways.

They are fairly high in calories, about 130 per cup. They are also rich in potassium, and a good source of Vitamin C.

But, before you can cook a plantain, you must peel it. Here

is an easy method.

## TROUBLE PEELING YOUR PLANTAIN?

While bananas are easy to peel, plantains, especially at their green, unripe stage, are a little more difficult. This is because the skin is thick and tends to cling to the meat inside.

1. Slice off the ends of the plantain, about 1/2 inch from the end, with a sharp paring knife. Throw the ends away.

2. Cut the plantain in half vertically.

3. With a sharp knife, make four evenly spaced cuts lengthwise into the plantain. Take care to cut through the skin and a bit of the plantain itself.

4. Take a corner of each slit in thumb and forefinger and lift the skin away, one strip at a time. It is easier to pull crosswise, rather than lengthwise.

5. Now you are ready to cook your plantain.

## BOILED PLANTAIN

**2 green plantains, peeled**
**1/2 teaspoon salt**
**2 tablespoons margarine**

Place plantains in saucepan and cover with water. Cook until tender, about 20 to 25 minutes. Serve hot, sprinkle with salt and dot with margarine.

Makes 4 servings: 160 calories, 6 grams fat, 0 milligrams cholesterol and 336 milligrams sodium.

# MASHED PLANTAIN

**2 green plantains, peeled**
**1/2 teaspoon salt**
**Pepper**
**3 tablespoons margarine**
**3 tablespoons canned evaporated milk, undiluted**

Boil plantains until tender, then drain. Mash with a fork or a potato masher. Add margarine, milk, salt and pepper and continue to mix well.

Makes 4 servings: 201 calories, 10 grams fat, 3 milligrams cholesterol and 382 milligrams sodium.

# FRIED RIPE PLANTAINS

**2 ripe plantains, peeled**
**Vegetable oil**
**Salt and pepper, to taste**

Cut plantains diagonally into 1 inch slices. Or, cut peeled plantain into thirds or fourths diagonally, depending on size of plantain, then each portion in half lengthwise.

To fry plantain in a frying pan, pour enough oil into the pan to lightly coat the bottom. Heat oil, then fry plantain until golden brown. Turn slices over and cook on underside until brown. Remove cooked slices to a serving platter and sprinkle with salt and pepper.

To fry plantain in the oven, coat a baking sheet lightly with oil. Place sliced plantain on oiled sheet and into a pre-heated 350 degree oven. Bake until browned and tender, about 15 to 20 minutes on each side. Remove cooked plantain to a serving platter and sprinkle with salt and pepper.

Makes 4 servings. Per serving: 154 calories, 5 grams fat, 0 milligrams cholesterol and 270 milligrams sodium.

## A STUFFING ALL IT'S OWN

"I learned to make West Indian Potato Stuffing about 20 years ago," said St. Thomas resident Amy Colon. "It goes with almost any dish but fish. I usually serve it with meat or fowl."

Many people are surprised by the sweet, yet spicy flavor of this dish. They also assume that sweet potatoes give the stuffing its dark orange-brown flavor. Wrong. It's the tomato paste and hot sauce which are the secret ingredients. These, combined with such other surprising ingredients like raisins and olives, makes this flavorful recipe a truly unique one.

## AMY'S WEST INDIAN POTATO STUFFING

**3-1/3 cups instant potato flakes**
**1/2 large green pepper, seeded and minced**
**1 stalk celery, minced**
**1/2 medium onion, minced**
**1 garlic clove, minced**
**2 tablespoons butter**
**1/2 cup tomato paste**
**3/4 cup seedless raisins**
**6 medium pitted black olives (optional)**
**1/4 cup white sugar**
**1 to 2 teaspoons hot sauce, or to taste**
**Black pepper to taste**
**1/4 to 1 cup fine bread crumbs**
**1 egg**

Make instant mashed potatoes from flakes, following package directions. Set aside.

Melt butter in a deep saucepan. Add green pepper, celery, onion and garlic. Stir in tomato paste, raisins and olives, if desired. Add sugar, hot sauce and black pepper, to taste. Add enough bread crumbs to thicken mixture. Add egg and mix well.

Combine vegetable mixture with potatoes and pour into a baking pan. Bake at 350 degrees for one hour.

Makes 12 servings. Per serving: 177 calories, 5 grams fat, 25 milligrams cholesterol and 312 milligrams sodium.

### SOUTHERN ITALY'S FRESH TOMATO DISHES

"We use lots of seafood and many dishes with tomatoes," explained Massimo Celentano, Chef/Owner at the *Piccola Marina Cafe*. Celentano is from the isle of Capri, where the food is richly southern Italian.

In addition to his fresh homemade pizzas fragrantly baked in a wood burning oven fueled by oak, one of Celentano's most popular menu items is Penne Alla Caprese.

Recipes for Virgin Island adaptations of northern and central Italian favorites are found on pages 123 and 146 respectively.

## PENNE ALLA CAPRESE

**Tomato Sauce:**
**1/2 chopped onion**
**2 tablespoons olive oil**
**1-1/2 pounds peeled tomatoes**
**20 fresh basil leaves**
**1/2 teaspoon salt**
**pepper, to taste**
**1/4 pound shredded mozzarella cheese**
**8 fresh basil leaves**
**1 pound Penne (short pasta)**

To make the tomato sauce, saute the onions in olive oil until the onions are golden. Add the peeled tomatoes and let cook for 30 minutes. Add basil leaves and salt and pepper, to taste. Stir and make sure to mash the tomatoes. Put the tomato sauce in a pan with the mozzarella cheese and fresh basil leaves. Add the cooked pasta. Toss for a few minutes and serve.

Makes 4 servings. Per serving: 329 calories, 13 grams fat, 54 milligrams cholesterol and 550 milligrams sodium.

## DOCOUNA

St. Johnians recently got a delightful surprise during a food fair at the Elaine I. Sprauve Museum in Cruz Bay. Local cook Hercules, of *Hercules Pate Delight*, made his delicious Docouna.

Docouna is a dumpling-like food made from a base of sweet potato and pumpkin which is then sweetened with brown sugar and coconut. Traditionally, the ingredients were wrapped in a leaf, a banana leaf, for example, before cooking. (When fresh leaves are not available, the ingredients can be wrapped in aluminum foil).

Either hot or cold, docouna tastes great eaten by itself or served with a plate full of stewed saltfish.

## HERCULES' "DOCOUNA" DELIGHT

**1 large or 2 small sweet potatoes, peeled (approx. 1 lb.)**
**3/4 cup coarsely chopped fresh pumpkin, peeled**
**1-1/4 cup grated dried coconut**
**1/2 cup firmly packed brown sugar**
**1 cup milk**
**1/2 cup flour**
**a pinch black pepper**

In a blender or food processor, grind together sweet potato and pumpkin. Place ground ingredients into a large mixing bowl. Add coconut, brown sugar, milk, flour and black pepper. Ingredients should make a stiff paste.

Fill a large pot with water and bring to a boil. Take sweet potato mixture and shape in the palm of the hand into small ovals or oblong pieces. The ovals should be a little larger than a quarter in size and the oblong pieces should measure about a hand's length. Wrap shaped portions in aluminum foil and boil for about 30 minutes.

Makes 12 oval size docouna. Per serving: 95 calories, 2 grams fat, 3 milligrams cholesterol and 20 milligrams sodium.

## DANISH-STYLE ASPARAGUS PUDDING

Gertrude Melchior knows several old-time recipes that date to the days when the Virgin Islands were owned by Denmark. Danish-Style Asparagus Pudding is one of them.

For two other of Melchior's family recipes see page 164 for her famous Wedding Cake and page 124 for her festive Croustades Filled with Creamed Chicken.

**1/2 cup flour**
**1/2 cup butter**
**1-1/4 cups milk**
**5 eggs, separated**
**1/2 teaspoon salt**
**2 teaspoons sugar**
**Black pepper, to taste**
**1 pound fresh asparagus,**
    **trimmed, cooked, and**
    **cut into bite-sized pieces**
    **(or equivalent quantity canned)**

Make a white sauce with the flour, butter and milk. Cool, then add egg yolks, stirring well. Flavor with salt, sugar and black pepper, to taste. Beat egg whites until stiff, then fold into white sauce.

In a greased baking dish, place alternate layers of sauce and asparagus. Bake in a 350 degree oven for 35 to 40 minutes, or until mixture is firm.

Makes 8 servings. Per serving: 216 calories, 16 grams fat, 169 milligrams cholesterol and 310 milligrams sodium.

## A CLASSIC FAVORITE - VIRGIN ISLANDS STYLE

Miriam Martin learned to cook from one of the Virgin Islands best-known cooks, Mildred A. Anduze.

In the early part of this century, Anduze taught young girls cooking and sewing. "Mrs. Anduze used to say that she could relax while sewing upstairs if she knew I was downstairs doing the cooking," Martin said.

At the age of 15, Martin made her professional cooking debut while working for a friend who owned a guest house. After she was married, Martin and her family moved to New York City. For over 15 years, she worked in the Dietary Departments of various New York hospitals.

When she returned to the Virgin Islands, she was quickly hired by the St. Thomas Hospital.

Whenever there was a special function at the hospital, Martin was chosen as head cook. When the Hemodialysis patients held their yearly Christmas Party, Martin made sure their low-salt dishes were as tasty as any. She loved to cook basic dishes with good old-fashioned flavor. Upon her retirement in 1989, Martin was given a special award by the hospital for her many accomplishments.

Of all the dishes she has made, many considered her Macaroni & Cheese a classic.

# MIRIAM MARTIN'S MACARONI & CHEESE

**6 cups cooked elbow macaroni (approx. 1 lb. dry)**
**3 cups Half & Half cream**
**1/2 pound cheddar cheese, shredded**
**1/4 pound butter**
**2 eggs, beaten**

Grease a large Pyrex baking dish. Add hot, cooked macaroni. Pour cream over macaroni. Stir in cheese, butter and eggs. Mix all ingredients well. Bake in a pre-heated 350 degree oven for 45 minutes, or until brown on top.

Makes 8 servings. Per serving: 384 calories, 26 grams fat, 118 milligrams cholesterol and 326 milligrams sodium.

# BREADS & BAKED GOODS

### 1. Sweet Potato Fritters

### 2. Pumpkin Fritters

### 3. Papaya Fritters

### 4. Johnny Cakes

### 5. Sweet Cassava Bread

### 6. Dumb Bread

### 7. Dorothy Elskoe's Christmas Sweet Bread

## HOT, CRISPY FRITTERS

Blanche Mills knows her way around a kitchen. She teaches the Food & Nutrition Program at the University of the Virgin Islands Cooperative Extension Service on St. Thomas.

"We help families to get good buys for their dollar, plan meals, make grocery lists, prepare and store food correctly, understand the nutritional value of food, use and prepare foods in different ways——and to cook easy, nutritious and delicious meals," Mills said.

A favorite recipe of Mills is for fritters. "Fritters can be flavored with sweet potato, pumpkin, papaya, banana or saltfish," she said

Here are three of Mill's fritter recipes and a bit of information about the tropical foods which flavors each.

## ABOUT BATATA OR TROPICAL SWEET POTATOES

Tropical sweet potatoes——or batata as they are called in Spanish——differ from the sweet potatoes found on the U.S. mainland. Their skin can be pink, pale yellow, cream color or reddish brown and their inner flesh can be white, light pink, yellow or bright orange. They are occasionally mistaken for yams.

The texture of the tropical sweet potato's flesh is similar to a mealy white potato. Its flavor is mildly sweet.

If tropical sweet potatoes are not available, then the North American variety of yam will substitute nicely in the following recipe for Sweet Potato Fritters.

In addition to making fritters, tropical sweet potatoes are often served boiled, baked or mashed as a starchy side dish to accompany a meat or fish entree. They can also be cut into chunks and added to soups or made into a sweet pudding with the additions of brown sugar, cinnamon and nutmeg.

A cup of sweet potato provides 230 calories. It also has a good amount of dietary fiber, Vitamin A, and potassium.

## SWEET POTATO FRITTERS

**2 cups peeled, grated sweet potato**
**1/2 cup sugar**
**1/4 teaspoon salt**
**1 teaspoon vanilla essence**
**1-1/2 teaspoons baking powder**
**1 cup milk**
**2 ripe bananas, peeled and crushed**
**1/2 cup all-purpose flour**
**1/4 cup grated coconut, if desired**
**Oil, for deep-fat frying**

Combine all ingredients until just mixed. Do not use an electric mixer and do not over mix. Drop by teaspoons into hot oil. Cook for 1 to 2 minutes on each side. Drain on paper towels. Fritters can also be cooked on a grill similar to a pancake. Serve hot as a snack or as an accompaniment to stewed saltfish.

Makes 12 fritters. Per fritter: 155 calories, 6 grams fat, 3 milligrams cholesterol and 104 milligrams sodium.

## ABOUT THE WEST INDIAN PUMPKIN - CALABAZA

Like the tropical sweet potato, the West Indian pumpkin (or calabaza) varies from the North American Halloween variety. In shape, it is usually more oval then round. In color, it has a greenish skin flecked with yellow or white blotches. The flesh inside is mildly sweet to taste, and is yellow to orange in color.

When West Indian pumpkin is not available, use hubbard or butternut squash in its place.

The West Indian pumpkin can be boiled, baked, or mashed.

It is often served as a side dish either plain or flavored with brown sugar and cinnamon. It can also be made into soup with (or without) the addition of other ingredients as ham, dumplings, onion, garlic, and black pepper.

A cup of pumpkin provides only 35 calories. It is an excellent source of Vitamin A, and a fair source of potassium, Vitamin C, and dietary fiber.

## PUMPKIN FRITTERS

**1-1/2 cups mashed pumpkin**
**1/4 cup sugar**
**1/4 teaspoon salt**
**1 teaspoon vanilla essence**
**1 teaspoon baking powder**
**1-1/4 cup milk**
**1 cup all-purpose flour**
**Oil, for deep-fat frying**

To make mashed pumpkin from fresh, begin by cutting a whole pumpkin in half lengthwise. Remove seeds and stringy fibers from center. Cut pumpkin into quarters. Place in a large pot and cover with water. Bring to a boil, reduce heat, and simmer 25 to 30 minutes until pumpkin flesh is fork tender. Drain water and scoop out pumpkin flesh from outer shell. Mash with a fork. One quarter of a medium-sized pumpkin yields approximately 1-1/2 cups mashed pumpkin.

In a mixing bowl, combine pumpkin, sugar (instead of adding sugar to the batter, it may be sprinkled over hot fritters after cooking), salt, vanilla, baking powder, milk and flour and stir until ingredients are just combined. Do not use an electric mixer and do not over mix.

Drop by teaspoonfuls into hot oil and fry 1 to 2 minutes on each side. Drain on paper towels. As another option, fritters can also be cooked on a griddle, similar to a pancake. Serve fritters

hot as a snack or side dish to a meal.
    Makes 12 fritters. Per fritter: 115 calories, 6 grams fat, 3
milligrams cholesterol and 86 milligrams sodium.

## ABOUT PAPAYAS

    Papaya can be eaten when unripe (green) or ripe
(yellow-orange), hot or cold, and as a vegetable or dessert. A
slightly unripe papaya, whose skin is greenish-yellow or
greenish-orange, is best for making Papaya Fritters. For a recipe
using green, unripe papaya, see page 55.
    A fully ripe papaya can be eaten out of your hand like a
melon. A squeeze of fresh lime greatly enhances its flavor.
Diced chunks of ripe papaya can be added to fruit, poultry and
seafood salads. The flesh can also be whirled in a blender with
crushed ice for a refreshing drink.
    A cup of papaya provides only 55 calories. It is an excellent
source of Vitamin A and C, plus potassium. It also offers a fair
amount of dietary fiber.

## PAPAYA FRITTERS

**1 cup self-rising flour**
**1/2 cup milk**
**1 egg, beaten**
**1-1/2 tablespoons sugar**
**1 cup papaya, peeled**
      **and cut into cubes**
**Oil, for deep-fat frying**

    Combine flour, milk, egg and sugar. Then, stir in papaya. Do
not use an electric mixer and do not over mix. Drop by
teaspoonfuls into hot oil. Cook 1 to 2 minutes on each side or
until golden brown. Drain on paper towels. Fritters can also be
cooked on a grill, similar to a pancake. Serve hot as a snack or

side-dish for a meal.

Makes 8 fritters. Per fritter: 104 calories, 3 grams fat, 28 milligrams cholesterol and 214 milligrams sodium.

## JOHNNY WAS A TRAVELER

Johnny Cakes are synonymous with Virgin Islands. They're for sale everywhere, and can be eaten as a snack or a meal.

These round or square, baked or fried, flour cakes were originally called "journey cakes." They were a food that could be prepared quickly and held up well during land or sea travel.

One of the best places to sample a johnny cake is at the *M & D Mobile* food van, located in Charlotte Amalie near Emancipation Garden. Maudlyn Frederick makes them fresh daily, starting the dough each morning at 3 AM. "They are my trademark——my secret," Frederick said.

Johnny Cakes are best eaten hot. Virgin Island residents especially love Johnny Cakes with fried local fish or stewed salted codfish.

Here is my favorite Johnny Cake recipe:

## JOHNNY CAKES

**2 cups flour**
**2 teaspoons baking powder**
**1 teaspoon sugar**
**1 teaspoon salt**
**2 tablespoons shortening**
**1/3 cup water (warm)**
**Oil, for deep-fat frying**

Combine flour, baking powder, sugar and salt in a mixing bowl. Add the shortening and mix until ingredients resemble coarse crumbs. Add water and mix until a smooth stiff dough forms. Knead thoroughly but lightly, until all lumps have disappeared. Place dough on a floured board and cover with a damp towel. Let rest 30 minutes.

In a deep saucepan, pour in oil to a depth of 3 to 4 inches and heat. Roll small pieces of dough into balls and flatten. Or, roll out dough to a 1/4 to 1/2-inch thickness and cut into squares. Fry johnny cakes on both sides until golden brown. Drain on paper towels.

As an alternative option, johnny cakes can be baked on an oiled baking sheet. Bake in a pre-heated 350 degree oven for 15 to 20 minutes or until golden brown. Baking will reduce both fat and calories in johnny cakes prepared this way.

Makes 12 Johnny Cakes.

Per fried Johnny Cake: 111 calories, 4 grams fat, 0 milligrams cholesterol and 234 milligrams sodium.

Per baked Johnny Cake: 91 calories, 2 grams fat, 0 milligrams cholesterol and 234 milligrams sodium.

## CASSAVA - FOOD OF THE PAST & PRESENT

The Arawak Indians inhabited the Caribbean islands long before Columbus. One of their staple foods was manioc, which we refer to today as cassava.

Cassava is easily grown and highly nutritious. A cup contains 270 calories. It is a good source of iron and fiber.

The Arawaks prepared cassava for bread baking by first scraping off its brown hairy husk. Then, they grated the white inner flesh and spooned it into a cloth. Finally, with the cloth firmly closed around the casssava, they squeezed out the juice. The remaining dry cassava was called cassava meal.

(Note: uncooked cassava juice is poisonous. It contains hydrocyanic acid. However, boiling evaporates this acid. The thick sauce which results from boiling cassava is known as cassareep. This is the principal flavoring agent in a dish called Pepperpot. Recipes for both cassareep and pepperpot are found on page 103).

The Arawaks baked their bread by placing a clay griddle over an open fire. They poured the cassava meal on top of this griddle. The heat slowly caramelized the cassava's natural sugars, gluing the meal together to make a thin, circular golden brown bread.

Making cassava bread by modern means does not detract from its flavor. In fact, innovations like the additions of shredded coconuts and brown sugar makes a tasty version called Sweet Cassava Bread.

## SWEET CASSAVA BREAD

**2 cups finely grated cassava**
**1 teaspoon salt**
**1/2 cup dried shredded coconut**
**1/2 cup brown sugar**

Mix the cassava and salt. Place in a damp kitchen towel or cloth and wring out all the liquid. (Save the liquid for Cassareep, recipe on page 104.)

Spread half of the cassava meal in the bottom of a small iron frying pan or other heavy frying pan and pat down firmly. Cover with the coconut and the brown sugar. Add the rest of the cassava and pat down lightly. Bake in a 350 degree oven until lightly browned or about 20 minutes.

Makes 6 servings. Per serving: 254 calories, 4 grams fat, 0 milligrams cholesterol and 118 milligrams sodium.

### DUMB BREAD TASTES SMART

Why are those round hearty loaves of crusty island local bread called 'dumb' bread?

"Dum refers to a style of cooking used in India to make bread," said Arona Petersen, a local food expert and author of *Food & Folklore of the Virgin Islands.* "Their cooking methods were similar to ours. They cooked bread on coal pots too. Over the years, this named got changed to dumb."

Dumb bread is a dense bread that is cut in wedge shaped slices. It can be eaten either plain, with butter, or filled with cheese. It is especially delicious right out of the oven.

## LOCAL ISLAND DUMB BREAD

**3-1/3 cups all-purpose flour**
**2/3 cup water**
**1/3 cup sugar**
**2 tablespoons evaporated milk**
**1/3 cup margarine or butter**
**1/3 cup shortening**
**3 tablespoons baking powder**
**4 tablespoons dried shredded**
    **coconut, if desired**

In a large mixing bowl, combine all ingredients to form a dough. On a floured surface, knead the dough until smooth, or about 10 to 15 minutes. (Dough will be somewhat stiff.)

Roll into a ball, then flatten slightly with the palm of the hand. Place loaves on a greased baking sheet. Bake in a pre-heated 350 degree oven for 35 to 40 minutes or until browned. Let cool briefly, then cut into ten wedges.

Makes 10 servings. Per serving (with coconut): 272 calories, 11 grams fat, 2 milligrams cholesterol and 388 milligrams sodium.

## TRADITIONAL CHRISTMAS SWEET BREAD

What flavor is Christmas?

"Guavaberry liqueur, boiled ham, salt beef, and sweet bread have long been associated with the Christmas holidays," said Virgin Island native Dorothy Elskoe. "I've been making sweet bread since I was 11 years old."

Even today, Elskoe maintains a rigorous schedule during the holidays. Baking sweet bread isn't easy—it is a time-consuming process.

## DOROTHY'S CHRISTMAS SWEET BREAD

1-1/2 teaspoons yeast
1/3 cup warm water
14 cups flour
2-1/2 teaspoons baking powder
1 cup firmly packed brown sugar
1 cup margarine or butter
1 egg

1/4 cup evaporated milk, warmed
1/2 teaspoon vanilla essence
1/4 teaspoon lemon essence
1/4 teaspoon lime peel
1/4 teaspoon cinnamon
1/2 teaspoon almond essence
pinch nutmeg

2/3 cup raisins
1/3 cup currants
2/3 cup mixed dried fruits
1/3 cup dried prunes
2 tablespoons guavaberry liqueur
   (* The recipe for homemade
guavaberry liqueur is on page 26.)

In a small mixing bowl, dissolve yeast in 2 tablespoons of the warm water. Sift 2 tablespoons of flour with baking powder. Add 1/4 teaspoon brown sugar, plus the sifted flour and baking powder mixture to the dissolved yeast and water. This makes the leaven. Put the leaven in a warm area of the kitchen to rise.

Cream butter and remaining brown sugar. Beat in egg.

Add butter, sugar and egg mixture to the leaven. Add a little warm milk a bit at a time, alternately with the flour, until batter is stiff. Flour dried fruits, saving a few not floured to decorate the top of the bread. Add floured fruits to batter with spices. Add the remaining water, milk, and guavaberry liqueur. Again, the batter should be stiff. Grease a large round cake pan and coat with flour. Fill pan about three-quarters full. Brush top with a brown sugar syrup. Decorate top with dried fruits. Place batter in a warm area of the kitchen and let rise until double in size.

Bake in a 350 degree oven for 45 minutes or until a knife inserted in it comes out clean.

Makes 1 sweet bread. Per 1/12 slice of sweet bread: 417 calories, 17 grams fat, 29 milligrams cholesterol and 305 milligrams sodium.

# SOUPS

1. Gazpacho

2. Kallaloo

3. Goat Water

4. Cactus Soup

5. Red Pea Soup (and Dumplings)

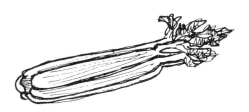

## LIMM'N ON ST JOHN

The island of St. John, which is nearly two thirds National Park, is only twenty minutes from St. Thomas by ferry. It's main town is the picturesque, quaint village of Cruz Bay. Within the small, quiet confines of this friendly little town are a number of fine restaurants and specialty shops.

Nestled back from one of the main streets is Chris and Rich Meyer's *Lime Inn*. The name of the restaurant is more imaginative than it appears, for "limin'" is the local term for relaxing. And the Meyer's hope that is exactly what their guests will do.

As transplanted US mainlanders, Chris and Rich fell in love with St. John on their first visit. They quickly decided to call the island their home, establish their business, and raise a family.

Wednesday night is their popular all-the-shrimp-you-can-eat feast at *Lime Inn*. Chris's spicy Gazpacho Soup makes a light, yet robust flavored appetizer before this grand seafood indulgence.

# GAZAPACHO SOUP

**2 16-ounce cans whole peeled tomatoes**
**1/2 medium red onion**
**1 green pepper, seeded**
**1 tablespoon paprika**
**1 teaspoon salt**
**1/4 cup bread crumbs**
**1/2 teaspoon fresh garlic**
**3 cups tomato or vegetable (V-8) juice**
**1/2 cup water**
**1/4 cup vegetable oil**
**1/4 cup balsamic vinegar**
**3 medium cucumbers, peeled, seeded and chopped**
**Sour cream or low fat yogurt, for garnish**

Process canned tomatoes, red onion, green pepper, paprika, salt, bread crumbs and garlic in a food processor or finely chop vegetables and add remaining ingredients.

In a large bowl, whisk together the tomato or vegetable juice, water, oil and vinegar. Add processed vegetable mixture to liquid ingredients. Add cucumbers. Serve gazpacho with a very cold dollop of sour cream or plain low fat yogurt on top.

Makes 8 servings. Per serving: (topped with one tablespoon sour cream) 196 calories, 10 grams fat, 6 milligrams cholesterol and 826 milligrams sodium.

Per serving: (topped with one tablespoon plain low-fat yogurt) 163 calories, 7 grams fat, 2 milligrams cholesterol and 905 milligrams sodium.

## GOOD EATING FOR OLD YEAR'S NIGHT

"Kallaloo is for good luck in the New Year, especially for lovers," said Arona Petersen, local food expert and author of *Food and Folklore of the Virgin Islands.* "The old folks said that if you served kallaloo to your loved one on Old Year's Night, there would be a wedding by June."

How did kallaloo become the traditional Old Year's Night meal?

"It all started with a ham bone," Petersen said. "By old year's day, all that would be left of the ham served on Christmas would be the bone. Most of the other ingredients in kallaloo were those that could be found growing outside or at the market, like spinach, okra and herb seasonings."

"Mostly," she continued, "kallaloo was a common pot. Some one would contribute the ham bone, someone else the fish or crab, and yet another person the greens. It was a dish to share with neighbors."

## ARONA PETERSEN'S KALLALOO

1/2 pound salted meat - pigtail,
   salt beef or pig mouth
water
small ham bone
1 (10 oz.) package frozen cut okra
1/2 large onion
1/4 bunch of seasoning (chervil,
   thyme, celery, parsley)
1 cloves garlic
1/2 hot pepper
1/2 pound boned fish, flaked
1 (10 oz.) package frozen
   chopped spinach
Sprig of balsam
Fungi

Soak salted meat in water for a few hours. Wash and put meat into a covered pot with enough water to cover meat. Bring water to a boil. Lower heat and cook until tender. Remove meat from water and set aside. Taste water that meat has been cooked in to make sure it's not too salty. Add fresh water until pot is more than half full. Put in ham bone and okra. Add onions, seasoning, garlic, hot pepper, boned fish and spinach. Let simmer for one to two hours until mixture has the consistency of a thick stew. Add more water if needed to prevent ingredients from burning. Cut meat into small pieces, return to the pot and simmer one hour longer. Add a sprig of garden balsam for the last half hour of cooking.

Serve with fungi.

Makes 8 servings. Per one cup serving: 155 calories, 2 grams fat, 43 cholesterol and 307 sodium.

## GOAT WATER IS ACTUALLY A HEARTY SOUP

Springtime in St. Thomas is Carnival time. The entire island celebrates. Calypso and steel pan bands march everywhere. Stilt-walking 'mocko jumbies' stalk the crowded, noisy streets. Huge parades, complete with colorfully colored costumed participants, tramp up and down the waterfront.

Of course, delicious food is everywhere.

For the last several years, Dorsett Martin has operated one of the many food booths in the Carnival Village. "It's hard work," Martin said, "but I love to cook."

Long into the night——with numerous friends and family members as helpers——Martin serves up hot, delicious dishes. Her varied menu includes tender whelks and rice, conch in onion butter sauce, fresh fish, crispy johnny cakes, and roasted chicken legs with sweet potato stuffing.

One of Martin's many special soups is her spicy Goat Water. Here is her recipe:

## DORSETT MARTIN'S GOAT WATER

**(Measurements are approximate)**
**5 pounds mutton**
**3 stalks celery, chopped**
**1 large sweet pepper,**
    **seeded and chopped**
**1 large onion, chopped**
**3 cloves garlic, chopped**
**1 teaspoon ground cloves**
**2 tablespoons tomato paste**
**2 stalks fresh thyme**
**4 tablespoons flour**
**Salt and hot pepper, to taste**

Wash mutton with vinegar. Trim off all fat from the meat and stew until tender. Mutton can be stewed the night before, then refrigerated. Once cold, any remaining fat will rise to the top and can be easily skimmed.

Place de-fatted cooked mutton in a large pot and add celery, sweet pepper, onion, garlic, ground cloves, tomato paste and enough water to cover the meat.

In a small pan, brown the flour. Add a little water to the flour to make a paste, then stir in the paste to the mutton and vegetable mixture. Simmer on low heat for about 30 minutes. Serve hot.

Makes 8 servings. Per serving: 548 calories, 29 grams fat, 189 milligrams cholesterol and 638 milligrams sodium.

## BRAVE THE THORNS - SAVOR THE SOUP

Many years ago, during Ivan and Doris Jadan's quest to live off the land, Doris found that green vegetables were hard to find during St. John's long, hot, dry season. Rather than resort to canned or frozen products, she began experimenting with the tender pads of the prickly pear cactus. Doris found that the soft, yet crunchy chunks of dethorned, chopped cactus pads made a wonderful soup——and resembled okra in texture and flavor.

For two more of Doris' delightful local recipes, look on page 48. The following is her special recipe for Cactus Soup:

# CACTUS SOUP

**1-1/2 pounds oxtail**
**Pond salt (\*)**
**Flour**
**3 to 4 tablespoons cooking oil**
**3 cans chicken broth**
**Water**
**3 leaves bay rum bush**
**1-1/2 cups cactus, chopped**
**1 yellowtail fish, poached**
**2 small onions, chopped**
**Dash hot pepper sauce**
**1 tin broken shrimp**
**1 12-ounce can V-8 juice**

Trim fat off oxtails. Salt the tails with pond salt, roll in flour and brown all sides in oil. This takes about 20 minutes. Use a large heavy fry pan.

Add chicken broth, plus 3 cans of water and bay rum leaves to the browned oxtails. Simmer or cook over low heat.

Add smooth, chopped cactus. Select tender young pads without woody fibers. It is necessary to simmer the cactus and oxtail in broth, covered, over low heat for 2 hours, until the meat will fall off the bones of the oxtails. During this long, slow cooking, drain off one cup of broth and poach or steam a yellowtail fish in the broth, plus a few drops of local hot pepper sauce. After 15 minutes, remove the fish and separate the fish from the bones. Add the fish and chopped onions to the big frying pan. Drain, rinse and add one tin of small broken shrimp.

After the cactus soup has simmered for 2 hours, add V-8 juice.

Makes approximately 18, 1-cup servings. Per serving (with 1 teaspoon pond salt for recipe): 186 calories, 7 grams fat, 77 milligrams cholesterol and 554 milligrams sodium.

(Note: parrotfish and yellowtail may contain the ciguatera toxin. Please refer to page 132 for an explanation of this potentially harmful element.)

## (*) POND SALT

There are several natural salt ponds in the Virgin Islands. The best are continuously exposed to strong winds to aid in the water's evaporation. The salt is usually harvested in late summer. Salt Pond Bay on St. John is a perfect example of just such a place.

What good is sea salt? Salt produced naturally from seawater contains many essential minerals which other salts may lack. (However, natural salt is still salt. If your doctor has advised you to avoid salt, sea salt should be avoided too.)

## THE BEST PEA SOUP IN THE VIRGIN ISLANDS

There are lots of different ways to make Red Pea Soup. Traditionally, this full-meal soup was made using small red beans like the California pink bean or Mexican chili bean. But, in the USVI, red kidney beans are most popular.

At St. Thomas' *Diamond Barrel Restaurant* in downtown Charlotte Amalie, Sheryl Penn makes Red Pea Soup the way she learned from her mother, Marilyn Penn. "It's a British tradition to flavor the soup with sugar," Penn said. "My mother is from Tortola."

Using dried kidney beans (instead of canned) and adding finely minced green pepper and onion are a few other secrets which Penn uses to make this soup one of the restaurant's best-selling menu items.

# THE *DIAMOND BARREL'S* RED PEA SOUP

1 (8 oz) package dried red kidney beans (1-1/4 cups)
4 cups water
1 salted pigtail, cut into small pieces
1 stalk celery, diced
1/4 cup parsley, chopped
1 sprig thyme, leaves removed from stems
 (or 1 teaspoon dried thyme)
1/2 green pepper, seeded and chopped fine
1/2 medium onion, chopped fine
2 tablespoons butter
Pinch salt
Black pepper, to taste
Dumplings (recipe follows)
1 medium sweet potato, peeled and cut into chunks
3 tablespoons sugar, or to taste

Soak dried kidney beans overnight in enough water to cover.
The next day, place soaked beans into a large soup pot and add 1 quart water. Bring beans and water to a boil. Reduce heat to a simmer and cook beans until tender, about two hours. Add pigtail, celery, parsley, thyme leaves, green pepper, onion, butter, salt and black pepper. Bring mixture to a simmer. Add uncooked dumplings and sweet potato. Continue simmering until sweet potatoes are soft, about 30 minutes. Add sugar right before serving.

Makes 4 servings.

Per serving (without dumplings): 395 calories, 11 grams fat, 23 milligrams cholesterol and 886 milligrams sodium.

Per serving (with 3 dumplings each from recipe below): 662 calories, 14 grams fat, 23 milligrams cholesterol and 1054 milligrams sodium.

## DUMPLINGS

These hearty dumplings are popular in Caribbean soups. In addition to Red Pea Soup, they are found in chicken soups, fish soups, beef soups, and soups made with variety meats like oxtail and bullfoot.

**2 cups flour**
**1 teaspoon salt**
**3 tablespoons fine yellow cornmeal**
**1 tablespoon margarine**
**Water**

In a large mixing bowl, combine flour, salt, cornmeal and margarine. Add about 1/4 cup water and begin to knead dough. Continue adding water, enough to make a stiff, not sticky dough. Roll dough out on a floured board and cut into small squares or rectangles.

Makes 12 small dumplings. Per dumpling: 89 calories, 1 gram fat, 0 milligrams cholesterol and 56 milligrams sodium.

# RED MEATS

1. Maultaschen

2. Danish Meatballs

3. Zigeuner Schnitzel

4. Kibbe Kabobs

5. Pepperpot (and Cassareep)

6. Meat Pate

7. Braised Pork & Red Lentils

8. Moimoi

9. Villa Morales Beef Stew (and Sofrito)

## SOUTHERN GERMAN COOKING

Rich, flavorful authentic German dishes are just one of the many European cuisines available locally. At the *Bavarian Restaurant & Pub* on St. Thomas, chef Jurgen Bitterwolf makes maultaschen—translated as 'mouth pockets'—as a special menu item.

"They are very common in the southern part of Germany where I am from," Bitterwolf said. "We eat much more pasta than do Germans from the north, who use more potatoes."

Bitterwolf recommends serving Maultaschen with roasted onions and a tossed green salad.

For a recipe from north Germany, see page 143.

## MAULTASCHEN

**2 cups flour**
**4 eggs**
**Pinch salt**
**4 onions**
**6 slices lean bacon, diced**
**1/2 pound ground meat (beef or pork)**
**8 ounces spinach, blanched and chopped**
**1/2 cup fresh chopped parsley**
**2 smoked bratwurst sausages, ground**
**Salt and nutmeg, to taste**
**Beef or chicken broth**

To make the dough, sift the flour onto a table. Add the eggs and salt. Knead enough to make a smooth and very firm dough. (Dough should resemble a pasta dough.) Cut dough into 6 pieces and roll them out paper thin.

To make the filling, saute onions and bacon. Combine sauteed onions and bacon with ground meat, spinach, parsley, bratwurst, salt and nutmeg. Spread filling on individual dough pieces. Fold dough over filling and press ends firmly together. Cut into 2-1/2 inch log pieces and close ends so that they will not open in the boiling process.

Place maultaschen in a saucepan filled with enough boiling broth to cover. Simmer until done, about 5 to 7 minutes. Remove maultaschen from broth and serve with roasted onions and salad.

Makes 6 servings. Per serving: 543 calories, 18 grams fat, 183 milligrams cholesterol and 672 milligrams sodium.

## THE DANISH INFLUENCE

Despite the fact that Denmark hasn't governed the Virgin Islands in almost a century, many Danish dishes are still popular today. Danish Meatballs, or Frikadellar, is a good example.

St. Thomas chef Bent Sorensen, who was born and raised in Denmark, says that the features which differentiate Danish meatballs from other nationalities are their ingredients, how they were made, and how they were shaped.

"Danish meatballs always contain a combination of pork and veal," Sorensen says. "When the meats are mixed with the other ingredients, air is 'slapped' into the mixture to give it a light texture when cooked."

The characteristic oblong, rather than oval, shape of Danish meatballs comes from the days when chefs would fashion the balls out of the palm of their hands, like they would make long, thin sausages.

"In place of oil, the meatballs should be sauteed in nothing other than pure Danish butter," Sorensen concluded.

# FRIKADELLAR (DANISH MEATBALLS)

**2-3/4 pound finely ground pork**
   **(or use half veal and**
   **half pork)**
**1-1/4 cup flour**
**2 tablespoon grated onion**
**2 teaspoon salt**
**3/4 teaspoon pepper**
**3 eggs, slightly beaten**
**1-1/2 cups low-fat milk**
**Danish butter, as needed**

In a large mixing bowl, blend meat, flour, onion, salt and pepper. Add eggs and mix well. Add milk, 1/2 cup at a time, letting the mixture absorb all the milk. Beat until almost fluffy. Cover and chill for one hour.

Melt butter in skillet over medium heat. Measure meatballs by rounded tablespoons, then pat into flat ovals. Brown in hot butter. Remove meatballs to a large baking sheet and bake at 350 degrees for 20 minutes.

Makes 12 servings, allowing 3 meatballs for each serving. Per serving: 273 calories, 13 grams fat, 127 milligrams cholesterol and 445 milligrams sodium.

## AUSTRIAN SCHNITZELS

Looking for a good Wiener Schnitzel? How about Jaeger Schnitzel or Zigeuner Schnitzel? These traditional Austrian favorites are just a few of the most popular dishes at *Alexander's Cafe* on St. Thomas.

Owner Alexander Treml, who was born and raised in Austria, explained that schnitzel is a thin piece of meat, usually veal, which has been tenderized by pounding. This tender veal is then used to make a variety of schnitzel dishes. Wiener Schnitzel is lightly breaded and pan-fried veal. Jaeger Schnitzel is veal with mushrooms served with a cream sauce. Zigeuner Schnitzel is prepared like this:

## ZIGEUNER SCHNITZEL

**3 tablespoons margarine**
**1 pound veal cutlets**
**Flour**
**1 large red pepper, cut in thin strips**
**1 large green pepper, cut in thin strips**
**1 large yellow pepper, cut in thin strips**
**1/2 large onion, cut in thin strips**
**8 ounces mushrooms, sliced**
**2 cloves garlic, minced**
**1 cup chicken stock**
**1 teaspoon freshly ground black pepper**

In a medium size saute pan, melt 1-1/2 tablespoons margarine. Pound veal cutlets with a mallet. Dredge veal in flour then place in hot saute pan and brown on both sides. When finished browning, remove veal to a separate plate.

Add peppers, onions, mushrooms, garlic and remaining 1-1/2 tablespoons margarine to the saute pan. Cook for five minutes until tender, yet crispy. Scrape all the meat residue from the bottom of the pan (this is where the flavor is!) while sauteing vegetables.

Add veal back with the vegetables. Add chicken stock and black pepper. Simmer for about 10 minutes or until the sauce thickens slightly.

To serve, place veal cutlets on individual plates, then top with sauteed vegetables. Veal is best accompanied by rice or potatoes and a fresh green vegetable.

Makes 4 servings. Per serving of veal: 236 calories, 8 grams fat, 89 milligrams cholesterol and 262 milligrams sodium.

## GROUND LAMB - MIDDLE EASTERN STYLE

"Depending where you are in the Middle East," said local cook Ed Sternberg, "this dish may be called kibbe kabobs, kufta kabobs or shish kibbeh."

Whatever the name, the dish is as popular in the Middle East as hamburgers are in the United States. Sternberg serves Kibbe Kabobs as one of forty-some dishes he makes each year during his special Christmas dinner. For another of his favorite recipes and a description of this fantastic meal, see page 119.

## KIBBE KABOBS

1-1/2 pounds ground lamb,
　　10 to 20% fat content
1/4 cup finely chopped fresh parsley
1/4 cup finely chopped onion
3 tablespoons finely ground bugler
　　wheat, soaked in water for
　　one hour and squeezed dry
　　(use a piece of muslin or old sheet
　　to wring out bugler)
3/4 teaspoon salt
1/4 teaspoon finely ground white pepper
1 heaping teaspoon cumin seed,
　　coarsely crushed with mortar
　　and pestle or 1/2 tsp ground cumin
1 to 2 tablespoons extra virgin olive
　　oil (omit oil if lamb is fatty)
Fresh lemon wedges
Plain yogurt or yogurt with fresh mint
Pita bread

Mix all ingredients together in a large bowl. Shape into sausage shapes which are 3/4" to 1" in diameter and 4" to 5" long. Refrigerate kabobs for 2 to 3 hours. Then, bake, broil or grill until done. Serve kabobs accompanied by slices of fresh lemon, plain or mint flavored yogurt and pita bread.

Makes 4 servings. Per serving (without lemon, yogurt or pita bread): 248 calories, 9 grams fat, 101 milligrams cholesterol and 480 milligrams sodium. Nutrient information for condiments are——one fresh lemon: 17 calories, 0 grams fat, 0 milligrams cholesterol and 1 milligram sodium. Two tablespoons plain low-fat yogurt mixed with dash of dried or fresh mint: 18 calories, 1 gram fat, 2 milligrams cholesterol and 20 milligrams sodium. One large pita bread: 105 calories, 0 milligrams fat, 0 milligrams cholesterol and 215 milligrams sodium.

## A TROPICAL STEW

Pepperpot is a rich stew which has is origins in Guyana, but which has also been made for hundreds of years throughout the Caribbean. The main flavoring agent in Pepperpot is Cassareep. For more information on cassava (from which cassareep is made) and for a recipe for Sweet Cassava Bread, see page 83, 104.

## PEPPERPOT

**1 pound oxtail**
**1 calf's foot, cleaned and cut into small pieces**
**1 pound pork loin, cut into bite-sized pieces**
**1 pound stewing beef, cut into bite-sized pieces**
**2 pounds chicken, cut into individual pieces**
**1/2 pound salted beef, cut into bite-sized pieces**
**2/3 cup cassareep (recipe follows)**
**1 fresh hot pepper**
**Salt to taste**

Combine all of the meats in a large heavy saucepan with enough water to cover all ingredients. Bring to a boil, then add the cassareep and the hot pepper. Reduce the heat and simmer for about 3 hours or until all the meats are tender and a thick gravy forms. Add salt to taste. Remove the hot pepper before serving. Serve over a bed of hot white rice.

Makes 8 servings. Per serving: 873 calories, 60 grams fat, 235 milligrams cholesterol and 618 milligrams sodium (without added salt).

## CASSAREEP

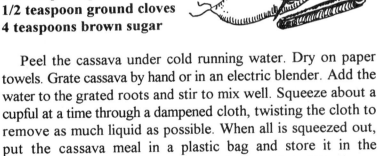

**4 pounds cassava**
**1 cup cold water**
**1/2 teaspoon ground cinnamon**
**1/2 teaspoon ground cloves**
**4 teaspoons brown sugar**

Peel the cassava under cold running water. Dry on paper towels. Grate cassava by hand or in an electric blender. Add the water to the grated roots and stir to mix well. Squeeze about a cupful at a time through a dampened cloth, twisting the cloth to remove as much liquid as possible. When all is squeezed out, put the cassava meal in a plastic bag and store it in the refrigerator for use in making Sweet Cassava Bread (recipe on page 83, 104).

Then, combine the liquid with the cinnamon, cloves and brown sugar. Bring to a boil, reduce the heat and simmer slowly, stirring from time to time, until the liquid is dark, thick and syrupy. Use to flavor pepperpot soup. Keep refrigerated.

Makes 1 cup. Per cup: 213 calories, 0 grams fat, 0 milligrams cholesterol and 14 milligrams sodium.

## PATE

In the Caribbean, a pate is a fried pastry filled with meat and/or vegetables. In 1988, the Daily New's 'Best of the Virgin Islands Awards' for the most delicious pate went to Augustus Beaupierre, owner of *Little Bopeep* restaurant on St. Thomas.

What makes his pate so special?

"It's the crust," Beaupierre said. "Most people don't know it, but the crust of a pate is as important as the crust of a pizza. It shouldn't be too hard or too soft."

Another special characteristic of a good pate is the quality of the ingredients used to make the filling. "I use only good quality beef," Beaupierre said. "That way, it's not too fatty. I also use up to sixteen different types of herbs and spices for seasonings."

At the *Little Bopeep* restaurants, Beaupierre sells pate made with beef, conch, chicken, shrimp, lobster, saltfish, and vegetable fillings. His beef pate is, by far, the most popular.

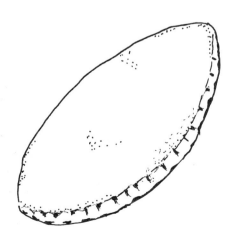

# *LITTLE BOPEEP* MEAT PATE

**Dough:**

**5 cups flour**
**1/4 cup vegetable shortening**
**2 tablespoons baking powder**
**1/4 to 1/2 cup water**

**Pate filling:**

**1/2 pound lean ground beef**
**1/2 small onion, chopped**
**1 small stalk celery, chopped**
**1/4 teaspoon salt**
**2 tablespoons green bell pepper, chopped**
**Dash oregano**
**Dash black pepper**
**1 teaspoon Kitchen Bouquet**
**2 teaspoons tomato paste**
**Dash parsley flakes**
**Dash garlic powder**
**1/4 small hot pepper, chopped (or to taste)**

To make dough: place flour, shortening, baking powder and water into a large mixing bowl. Add enough water to make a dough. Knead for 10 to 15 minutes. Let dough sit for 20 minutes.

To make ground meat filling: cook ground beef in a large frying pan with onion, celery, bell pepper, black pepper, garlic powder, oregano, parsley flakes, salt, tomato paste, Kitchen Bouquet and hot pepper. Continue cooking until ground beef is well cooked and vegetables are tender. Stir often while cooking to blend ingredients well. Use a large strainer to remove excess fat from the meat mixture.

Divide dough into 8 pieces. Roll flat and place 1-1/2 tablespoons of ground beef mixture in center of flattened dough. Fold dough over filling and use a fork to seal ends so that filling is completely sealed inside like a turnover. Use dough cutter to cut excess dough around the pate to give an even shape.

Deep fry in vegetable oil or shortening at 360 degrees until golden brown. Makes about 8 pate. Per pate: 418 calories, 11 grams fat, 15 milligrams cholesterol and 344 milligrams sodium.

## A TOUCH OF FRANCE IN THE VIRGIN ISLANDS

Actually, there is more than just a touch of France in the Virgin Islands. There is a large French community. This community is composed of people whose ancestors trace back many generations on St. Thomas, then to the island of St. Barts, and finally to France itself. French traditions and cuisine are very much alive here today.

*Cafe Normandie* is one of the many restaurants located in the Frenchtown section of St. Thomas. How did the name come about? "Many of our local residents trace their ancestors back to the Normandy region of France," says *Cafe Normandie's* owner/chef, George Johnson by way of explanation.

*Cafe Normandie* opened its doors in 1975, and has been serving fine french cuisine ever since. On the daily menu are fresh meat, poultry, and fish dishes. Their garden vegetables are particularly tasty. Of course, the crusty breads are home-baked.

In addition to the regular menu, Johnson prepares special dishes which are particular French favorites like squab, rabbit, tripe, and sweetbreads.

"Father's Day is a traditional holiday in Frenchtown," Johnson said. "We have people who wait all year long for the fresh snapper soup we serve."

"The new cooking in France," explains *Cafe Normandie's* Executive Chef William Wahl, "is working with the traditional base of foods, but giving more attention to the flavor of the ingredients and creating not such heavy sauces."

This new French cuisine is hallmarked by a near absence of roux (flour and butter based sauces). Instead, thickening and concentration of flavors is achieved by reduction or simmering over a slow fire until the mixture has diminished in bulk. Also, olive oil is used as a substitute for butter in many recipes.

"A good stock may have 10 to 15 hours of work in it," Wahl said. He starts with fresh seasonings and bones rather than a prepackaged base. About the time, he said, "It's a labor of love."

Braised Pork & Red Lentils is a popular dish at *Cafe Normandie*. Another of *Cafe Normandie's* popular recipes is the classic Coq Au Vin. See page 126.

## BRAISED PORK & RED LENTILS

**2 cups dried red lentils**
**2 shallots, finely chopped**
**2 tablespoons extra virgin olive oil**
**1 green pepper, seeded and chopped**
**1 medium onion, chopped**
**2 cloves garlic, finely**
**    chopped (add more to taste, if desired)**
**5 pound pork butt, trimmed of fat**
**    and cut into 2-inch cubes**
**3 bay leaves**
**1/2 cup water or white wine**
**2 tablespoons of red wine vinegar**
**Freshly ground black pepper, to taste**
**1 cup brown stock**
**Salt, to taste**
**Fresh chopped parsley, for garnish**

Soak red lentils in water overnight, then drain.

In a pot with a lid, heat olive oil and quickly saute green pepper, onion, shallots and garlic. Add pork cubes to pot with bay leaves, water or white wine, red wine vinegar and ground pepper. Place mixture in a pre-heated 400 degree oven and cook uncovered, for 10 minutes. Then cover and reduce heat to 350 degrees for 50 minutes. Add brown stock while cooking.

Prepare lentils by placing them and 4 cups of boiling water into a saucepan. Cover saucepan, reduce heat and simmer on low heat approximately 1-1/2 hours, or until lentils are tender. Drain. Add lentils to braised pork, add salt to taste and serve on a pre-heated dinner plate. Garnish with freshly chopped parsley. Makes 8 servings. Per serving (with 1/2 teaspoon salt used in recipe): 298 calories, 9 grams fat, 68 milligrams cholesterol and 182 milligrams sodium.

## THE CUISINE OF NIGERIA

The African influence has played the major role in shaping the cuisine in the Virgin Islands—and all other Caribbean islands as well. This is still going on today.

Take Olufunlayo E. I. Ladeloye as an example. She is from the Yorba region of Nigeria. She moved to the Virgin Islands recently, and is employed as a Registered Nurse at the St. Thomas Hospital. Some of the local foods in the Virgin Islands are familiar to her, others are not.

In her Nigerian homeland, Ladeloye said that the most frequently eaten foods are: bush meats (wild animals and birds), fresh water fish, home-grown birds, yam, cocoyam (tania), beans, peas, corn, maize, plantains, bananas, and many other fruits indigenous to the region.

A favorite dish served either for breakfast or for a light supper in the Yorba region is moimoi. Moimoi is a steamed pudding made from black-eyed peas which have various meats, fish and chopped hard-boiled egg neatly tucked into the center.

Ladeloye said that moimoi is served with a hot cereal pap called
ogi, which is made from various types of dried corn or maize.
Here is her recipe for moimoi:

# MOIMOI

**1 cup dried black-eyed beans**
**1/4 medium onion, chopped**
**3 tablespoons tomato puree**
**1/4 cup vegetable oil**
**dash of cayenne pepper or finely minced hot pepper**
**Salt, to taste**
**1 hard boiled egg, shelled and cut into quarters**
**1/4 cup canned corned beef, cut into bite-sized pieces**
**1/4 cup cooked tuna, flaked into bite-sized pieces**

Soak black-eyed peas in water for at least one hour. Rub
soaked beans between hands or in a colander to remove skins.
In a blender, grind beans, onion, tomato puree and oil. Add
cayenne or fresh hot pepper and salt to taste.

Traditionally, moimoi is spooned into banana leaves. When
leaves are not available, aluminum foil, carefully folded into
triangular-shaped packets can substitute. Foil should be
approximately 12"x 6".

Into the center of the foil packet, spoon a small amount of
the pea mixture. Then add a quarter of a hard-boiled egg, 1
tablespoon corned beef, and 1 tablespoon tuna. Spoon in
enough pea mixture to fill inside of foil packet. Wrap foil
packets carefully so they will be water tight, crimp edges to
seal.

In a deep saucepan, heat about 1 to 2 inches of water until
boiling. Place packets with moimoi into saucepan and cover
with a lid. Steam moimoi 25 to 30 minutes.

To serve, unfold moimoi from foil and place on a serving
dish.

Makes 4 servings. Per serving: 524 calories, 51 grams fat, 59 milligrams cholesterol and 268 milligrams sodium.

## THE INFLUENCE OF PUERTO RICO

Spanish explorers have had a great influence on local cuisine. Not only did the Spanish bring their own food to the islands, but they also brought foods from other regions. In addition, the Spanish colonists experimented with local ingredients and incorporated much of the tropical bounty into their diets.

Today, the cuisine of Puerto Rico, for example, has developed a richness of flavor and variety that is different from the traditional cooking in Spain. (For a look at traditional Spanish cooking in the islands, see page 148.)

In the Virgins, the island of St. Croix has an especially rich Puerto Rican cuisine. At *Villa Morales*, in Estate Whim, owner Angela Morales says that some of her most popular entrees are beef stew and roast pork accompanied by rice and pigeon peas or stewed red beans. One of her favorite ways of flavoring foods is with sofrito. "Sofrito is a s spicy sauce made with savory vegetables, herbs and spices," Morales said. "We use it both for flavor and color."

*Villa Morales* was started in 1964 by Morales' parents. As a teenager, she enjoyed helping in the kitchen. She took over the operation in 1976, and has been serving what she calls 'local Spanish cuisine' ever since. Enjoy *Villa Morales* Beef Stew seasoned with spicy Sofrito.

## *VILLA MORALES* BEEF STEW

**3 pounds beef, for stewing, cut in 1/2-inch cubes**
**Salt and pepper, to taste**
**3 tablespoons oil**
**3 tablespoons sofrito (recipe follows)**
**5 tablespoons tomato paste**
**6 cups water**
**2 potatoes, cut in cubes**
**2 carrots, diced**

Clean beef and season with salt and pepper. Use a thick pot with cover and heat the oil. Add sofrito and tomato paste. Stir and let cook for a few minutes on medium heat. Add meat and water. Stir and place the cover on pot. Increase heat and bring mixture to a boil. Then reduce heat and simmer for 1-1/2 to 2 hours. When beef is tender, add potatoes and carrots. Continue to simmer until potatoes are soft. Makes approximately 8 servings. Per serving: 399 calories, 23 grams fat, 103 milligrams cholesterol and 373 milligrams sodium.

## SOFRITO

**2 pounds small Puerto Rican**
**    sweet peppers**
**2 large onions**
**1 bulb garlic**
**1/4 cup oregano leaves**
**12 French thyme leaves (`re cao)**
**1/2 cup water**

Mix all ingredients in food processor. Sofrito can be frozen in an ice cube tray and used as needed. Makes approximately 4 cups. Per three tablespoon serving: 7 calories, 0 grams fat, 0 milligrams cholesterol and 1 milligrams sodium.

# POULTRY

**1. Twelve Clove Garlic Chicken**

**2. Roast Chicken with Native Seasoning**

**3. Middle Eastern Style Marinated Chicken**

**4. Chicken in Sherry Wine Vinegar**

**5. Chicken Piccante**

**6. Croustades with Creamed Chicken**

**7. Coq Au Vin**

**8. Chicken Cashew Nut**

## THE GIFT OF GARLIC

Fresh garlic's popularity as a seasoning, combined with its reputed medical benefits, makes it a food no kitchen should be without. Since 3000 BC, when it was used by the Babylonians, garlic has enjoyed the status of both flavoring and medicine.

As for it's medicinal benefits, scientists have discovered special chemical compounds that back up "old wive's tales" of garlic's healing capabilities.

For example, the compound, methyl allyl trisulfide is found in garlic. It can dilate blood vessels and help lower blood pressure.

An amino acid by-product in garlic, called allium (which is converted in the body to a substance called allicin) has antibacterial action equivalent to 1% of penicillin.

Garlic also has a reputation for treating colds, yeast infections, heart disease, arthritis, high blood cholesterol, and indigestion.

What about garlic as a food?

It tastes great in salads, vegetables, poultry, meat and fish dishes. Of course, make sure you use the real thing. One of the worst moves to make, flavor-wise, is to substitute garlic salt or garlic powder for fresh garlic. These powders just do not impart the same pungent flavor, and they can add a bitter or 'off' taste to a dish.

Another no-no when cooking with garlic is to saute it for the same length of time as onion. Garlic cooks faster than onion and will burn easily, giving the resulting dish a bitter flavor.

When cooked, garlic looses its raw, fiery flavor and becomes pleasantly mild. Cooked whole cloves of garlic make delicious eating, and are a delicious addition to combination dishes like Twelve Clove Garlic Chicken:

# TWELVE CLOVE GARLIC CHICKEN

**4 chicken breasts**
**1/3 cup flour**
**Salt and black pepper, to taste**
**1 tablespoon cooking oil**
**4 sprigs fresh thyme, or 1**
**    teaspoon dried thyme leaves**
**2 teaspoons fresh chopped rosemary**
**    leaves or 1 teaspoon  dried**
**12 cloves garlic, unpeeled**
**1 bay leaf**
**1/3 cup white wine**
**2/3 cup chicken broth**
**1/4 cup chopped fresh parsley**

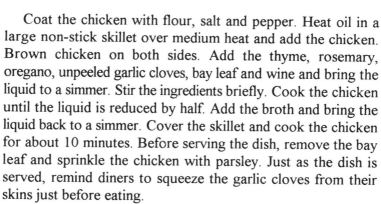

Coat the chicken with flour, salt and pepper. Heat oil in a large non-stick skillet over medium heat and add the chicken. Brown chicken on both sides. Add the thyme, rosemary, oregano, unpeeled garlic cloves, bay leaf and wine and bring the liquid to a simmer. Stir the ingredients briefly. Cook the chicken until the liquid is reduced by half. Add the broth and bring the liquid back to a simmer. Cover the skillet and cook the chicken for about 10 minutes. Before serving the dish, remove the bay leaf and sprinkle the chicken with parsley. Just as the dish is served, remind diners to squeeze the garlic cloves from their skins just before eating.

Makes 4 servings. Per serving (with skin on chicken and with 1 teaspoon salt used in recipe): 498 calories, 19 grams fat, 166 milligrams cholesterol and 560 sodium. Per serving (with chicken skin removed before cooking and with 1 teaspoon salt used in recipe): 408 calories, 9 grams fat, 145 milligrams cholesterol and 542 milligrams sodium.

## PERFECT POULTRY

Seasoning poultry to perfection is a West Indian art.

To prepare chicken for an evening meal, the cook must begin his/her preparation many hours (if not a day) in advance. First, the chicken must be washed with vinegar. This cleans the meat and removes any strong poultry odors. Then, the chicken must be properly seasoned.

The proper West Indian seasoning for chicken is an exotic mixture of the different ingredients. Aromatic onions, hot peppers, pungent parsley, savory thyme, and a wide vary of other spices are pounded with mortar and pestle (or in a modern blender or food processor).

Then this mixture is thoroughly rubbed into every part of the chicken. Next, the chicken is refrigerated for at least 8 to 12 hours or overnight. This allows the meat to absorb flavors. The result is out-of-this-world.

The following recipe for seasoning makes a large quantity. Store the extra seasoning in a container with a tight fitting lid in the refrigerator. It will stay good for several weeks——if it lasts that long!

# NATIVE SEASONING FOR CHICKEN

2 onions, coarsely chopped
1 tablespoon Accent
2 bunches scallion, chopped
1 pound box of salt
1 tablespoon poultry seasoning
1 tablespoon paprika
2 tablespoons black pepper
2 small hot peppers, seeds removed and chopped
1 bunch parsley, removed from stems and chopped
1 bunch celery, cleaned and chopped, including leaves
1 bunch fresh thyme, with stems removed
3 green peppers, seeded and chopped
3 heads garlic, peeled and coarsely chopped

With a blender or food processor, combine onion, scallion, hot pepper, parsley, celery, thyme, green pepper and garlic until finely blended, yet not liquified. Do not add water.

Place blended ingredients into a large mixing bowl. Stir in Accent, poultry seasoning, salt, paprika and black pepper. Place seasoning into a container with a tight fitting lid and store in the refrigerator.

To use seasoning, first wash poultry with vinegar. Then place poultry in a large baking pan and season with above mixture. Refrigerate seasoned poultry for at least ten hours to allow seasoning to impart its delicious flavor.

The above recipe makes about 5 cups of seasoning. Per one teaspoon seasoning: 2 calories, 0 grams fat, 0 milligrams cholesterol and 801 milligrams sodium (*).

* One teaspoon of ordinary salt contains: 2300 milligrams sodium.

## NUTRITIONAL CONTENT OF SEASONED CHICKEN

1 baked chicken leg seasoned with 1/4 tsp seasoning provides: 265 calories, 15 grams fat, 106 milligrams cholesterol and 301 milligrams sodium.

1 baked chicken leg (skin removed) seasoned with 1/4 tsp seasoning provides: 185 calories, 8 grams fat, 90 milligrams cholesterol and 288 milligrams sodium.

1 baked chicken breast seasoned with 1/4 tsp seasoning provides: 193 calories, 8 grams fat, 83 milligrams cholesterol and 269 milligrams sodium.

1 baked chicken breast (skin removed) seasoned with 1/4 tsp seasoning provides: 142 calories, 3 grams fat, 73 milligrams cholesterol, and 263 milligrams sodium.

1 baked chicken drumstick seasoned with 1/4 tsp seasoning provides: 112 calories, 6 grams fat, 48 milligrams cholesterol and 247 milligrams sodium.

1 baked chicken drumstick (skin removed) seasoned with 1/4 tsp seasoning provides: 76 calories, 3 grams fat, 41 milligrams cholesterol and 242 milligrams sodium.

1 baked chicken thigh seasoned with 1/4 tsp seasoning provides: 153 calories, 10 grams fat, 58 milligrams cholesterol and 252 milligrams sodium.

1 baked chicken thigh (skin removed) seasoned with 1/4 tsp seasoning provides: 109 calories, 6 grams fat, 49 milligrams cholesterol and 246 milligrams sodium.

1 baked chicken wing seasoned with 1/4 tsp seasoning

provides: 99 calories, 7 grams fat, 29 milligrams cholesterol and 228 milligrams sodium.

## A TRADITIONAL CHRISTMAS DINNER

There is no traditional turkey on Ed and Cathy Sternberg's Christmas table. But these long-time St. Thomas residents always have plenty for their guests to eat.

Every Christmas since the late 1970's, Ed Sternberg has orchestrated the preparation of 30 to 40 different traditional Middle Eastern dishes for up to 75 guests. He describes his feast as "what would have been served at the Bethlehem Hilton in the year zero."

This tradition, Sternberg said, began long ago when he lived in New York. He used to meet his wife, who was then a waitress in a Middle Eastern restaurant, for a late supper. Over the years, Syrian, Egyptian, Jordanian, Lebanese, and Persian friends would join them, and share recipes from their native lands. It is from these recipes that Sternberg prepares his Christmas dinner.

Adding authenticity to the meal, Sternberg does not use any prepared foods or cooking equipment or method that was not in use 2000 years ago. To accomplish this feast, Sternberg does not work alone. His co-chef is good friend Dean Barnes. Sternberg also gets help from his wife Cathy and mother Hansi. Cathy sees to the arrangement of the house and prepares the breads. Hansi bakes baklava and other sweet desserts. Dean, who was born and raised in Saudi Arabia, is Ed's right hand man when it comes to preparing the main dishes and numerous salads.

When the clock strikes 7 in the evening, the feast begins. Marinated Chicken, Syrian Style, is just one dish in the fabulous spread. Turn to page 102 for another of Sternberg's Middle Eastern favorites.

## MIDDLE EASTERN MARINATED CHICKEN

1 teaspoon ground coriander
1 teaspoon cumin
3 large cloves garlic
1/2 teaspoon dried oregano
1 tablespoon sesame tahini
1/2 teaspoon salt
1/4 teaspoon white pepper
1 ounce cold pressed olive oil
1 ounce vegetable oil
1 teaspoon mint, dried
1/2 cup fresh parsley, chopped
1/4 lemon, chopped
1/2 large Spanish onion, chopped

* * * * * *

1 small starchy potato
Dash lemon juice
1 teaspoon dried mint leaves, or to taste
4 boneless, skinless chicken
    breasts or one small chicken, cut
    into serving pieces

Make marinade by placing first 13 ingredients into blender and mixing well. Store in glass container and refrigerate. This marinade will keep 2 to 3 weeks when refrigerated. (You can add water, olive oil and lemon juice to the basic marinade ingredients for a delicious salad dressing.)

Peel, grate and blend potato until it becomes a fine pulp, without adding water. (Do not worry if potato discolors.)

Combine equal amounts of marinade and pulped potato. Add mint, lemon juice and mix well. Marinate chicken overnight in refrigerator.

The next day, pour off accumulated liquid and lay chicken on an oiled baking sheet. Bake in a 550 degree Fahrenheit oven or barbecue until chicken is crusty brown on the outside. This dish also works well on skewers with pieces of onion and green pepper in the shish kabob style.

Makes 4 servings. Per serving: 454 calories, 17 grams fat, 166 milligrams cholesterol and 176 milligrams sodium.

## CHEF PATRICK PINON DEFINES FINE CUISINE

He has been the Executive Chef at *Maxim's de Paris* and the *Russian Tea Room* in New York. He has even been the personal chef to Prince Bandar Bin Sultan of Saudi Arabia. Now, chef Patrick Alain Pinon is working his culinary magic locally, at the *Palm Terrace Restaurant* at the *Grand Palazzo Hotel.*

"The menu I created here is the result of my long experience working with many distinguished chefs world-wide," said Pinon.

Many of Pinon's best dishes are classic French recipes which he's redone to be fashionably light.

Chicken in Sherry Wine Vinegar is one of Pinon's most popular recipes. He recommends serving this entree with fresh slices of zucchini which have been sauteed in butter and seasoned with garlic, parsley, basil and diced tomatoes.

# CHICKEN IN SHERRY WINE VINEGAR

4-5 pound chicken, cut into serving pieces
Flour
1/2 cup butter
4 garlic cloves, finely chopped
1 onion, chopped
1/2 cup sherry wine vinegar
1/2 cup dry white wine
1 tablespoon tomato puree
Salt
Ground black pepper
2 cups veal stock or strong chicken stock
1 tablespoon Dijon mustard
4 sliced prosciutto ham (lean), cut into fine strips
8 large mushrooms cut julienne

Season and dredge chicken pieces in the flour. Shake off surplus flour. In a deep frying pan, melt half the butter. Add the chicken pieces and brown them lightly. Add garlic and onion, cooking with the chicken until translucent. Then add sherry vinegar, white wine, tomato puree and the veal stock or chicken stock. Season lightly with salt and pepper. The liquid must barely cover the chicken. Bring the mixture to a boil. Cover the pan and reduce the heat. Simmer, turning the chicken occasionally, for 20 to 25 minutes or until chicken is cooked. Transfer the chicken pieces to a serving dish. Skim the fat from the cooking liquid. If the flavor is weak, raise the heat to reduce the sauce and concentrate the flavor.

At the same time, blanch the prosciutto in boiling unsalted water for a few minutes. Strain and keep on the side.

In a small frying pan, melt a little butter. Add the mushrooms, seasoned lightly and sprinkle with a few drops of sherry vinegar. Saute quickly until all vegetable water has evaporated. Then add the prosciutto. Keep on the side.

Now remove the pan with the sauce from the heat and strain it into a small pan. Whisk in the remaining butter and the mustard to taste. Pour the sauce over the chicken and sprinkle with the mushroom and prosciutto garnish.

Makes 4 servings. Per serving: 544 calories, 20 grams fat, 191 milligrams cholesterol and 949 milligrams sodium.

## NORTHERN ITALIAN FARE - VIRGIN ISLAND STYLE

Not only can you find good Italian food here in the Virgin Islands——you can also find restaurants specializing in northern, central and southern Italian cuisine.

"Northern Italy boarders France," explained Willie Pelletier, Executive Chef at *Paradiso* in Cruz Bay, St. John. "Many of our dishes have light sauces. For example, our Tortellini Paradiso is served in a light garlic cream sauce. We also serve our linguine with clam sauce in either a red or white sauce."

In the recipe below, Pelletier flavors a simple sauteed chicken breast with a spicy, yet creamy and delicious sauce.

For recipes from central and southern Italy, see pages 146 and 71 , respectively.

# CHICKEN PICCANTE

**Picante Sauce:**

12 ounces heavy cream
5 cherry tomatoes, cut in half
1 jalapeno pepper, sliced
3 green olives, sliced
1/4 cup diced scallions
1/3 roasted red pepper, julienned
2 squirts Tabasco
1/2 ounce Worcestershire sauce
Olive oil
Cooked Linguine
1 hot cherry pepper, seeded and sliced
1 demi-tas spoon of Virgin Fire or Caribbean Hot Sauce
10 ounces chicken breast

To make the picante sauce, simmer heavy cream in a saucepan until reduced by one-third. To the reduced cream, add tomatoes, jalapeno pepper, olives, hot pepper, roasted red pepper, scallions, hot sauce, Worcestershire sauce and Tabasco. Continue simmering until some of the liquid evaporates and sauce thickens.

Saute chicken breast in olive oil, then bake in oven until done.

Pour picante sauce over chicken. Serve with a small side dish of cooked linguine and vegetable.

Makes 1 serving. Per serving (chicken, sauce and 1/2 cup linguine): 849 calories, 56 grams fat, 327 milligrams cholesterol and 598 milligrams sodium.

## OLD-TIME GOODNESS

Tiny crisp batter fried croustada shells are one of Gertrude

Melchior's favorite dishes. She makes them for special occasions all through the year, but especially at Christmas. "They can be filled with either creamed chicken, creamed oysters, or even creamed vegetables," Melchior explained.

The key to the croustada's unique shape lies in the old-fashioned cast iron mold from which they are made. "The closest I've seen today," Melchior said, "are the molds used to make timbales."

For two other of Melchior's old-time family recipes see page 164 for her Wedding Cake and page 73 for her Danish-Style Asparagus Pudding.

## CROUSTADAS WITH CREAMED CHICKEN

**Croustadas:**

**2 egg yolks**
**2 cups flour**
**2 teaspoons salt**
**1 cup beer**
**1 cup brandy**
**2 tablespoons melted shortening**
**Oil, for deep-fat frying**

Beat egg yolks slightly. Sift flour and salt. Add flour and salt alternately with beer and brandy. Add in melted shortening. Set mixture aside.

Meanwhile, heat oil in a wide frying pan or kettle. Dip croustada iron into heated oil until extremely hot. When hot, dip hot iron into batter. With batter clinging dip back into the hot oil and cook until slightly browned and crispy.

Fill cooled croustadas with hot creamed chicken.

Makes 32 croustadas. Per croustada shell: 31 calories, 1 gram fat, 13 milligrams cholesterol and 135 milligrams sodium.

**Creamed Chicken:**

2 tablespoons butter
2 tablespoons flour
1 cup milk
2 tablespoons freshly chopped parsley
1 teaspoon dry sherry
Salt and pepper, to taste
2 cups cooked chicken, finely chopped
6-ounce can sliced mushrooms, drained and chopped

In a saucepan, melt butter over low heat. Blend in flour and continue to stir for 3 to 4 minutes until smooth. Slowly stir in milk and continue stirring until mixture thickens.

To thickened sauce, stir in parsley, chicken and mushrooms. Add sherry, salt and pepper to taste. Spoon mixture into croustadas. Serve immediately.

Makes 2-3/4 cups. Per 2 tablespoon serving for filling croustadas: 38 calories, 2 grams fat, 14 milligrams cholesterol and 73 milligrams sodium.

Nutrient content for each cream chicken filled croustada: 69 calories, 3 grams fat, 27 milligrams cholesterol and 208 milligrams sodium.

## CLASSIC FRENCH FARE IN FRENCHTOWN

*Cafe Normandie*, located in the Frenchtown section of St. Thomas, has been serving delicious French foods for over a decade. Over the past few years, chefs George Johnson and William Wahl have lightened their classic fare in the style of new French cuisine.

Their recipe for Coq Au Vin, for example, is not made with a heavy flour and butter-thickened sauce. Instead, the 'slow simmering' of the dish imparts its unique flavor.

Another of *Cafe Normandie's* popular recipes, Braised Pork

& Red Lentils, is found on page 108.

## COQ AU VIN

**1 carrot, diced**
**3 shallots, diced**
**3 cloves garlic, chopped**
**1/2 cup onions, chopped**
**1 whole plump roasting chicken**
**3 tablespoons extra virgin olive oil**
**1/4 pound lean smoked ham, diced**
**1/2 cup Pearl onions, washed and drained**
**1/4 cup fresh parsley, chopped**
**1 tablespoon leaf oregano**
**3 bay leaves**
**1/2 tablespoon fresh thyme leaves**
**1 tablespoon brandy**
**Salt and pepper, to taste**
**1-1/2 cups dry red wine**
**1/2 pound fresh mushrooms, sliced**

Soak chicken in salted water for 1 to 2 hours. This will help remove excess blood. After soaking, remove chicken skin and de-bone, leaving drumsticks intact. Slice meat into serving portions.

In a large pot, add chicken parts and brown lightly with olive oil, ham, onions, Pearl onions, carrot, shallot and garlic. Then add parsley, oregano, bay leaves, thyme, brandy and salt and pepper, to taste. Mix well, then add red wine. Place lid on pot and simmer over low hat until done, or about one hour. During the last 5 minutes of cooking, add fresh mushrooms.

Serve chicken on a pre-heated dinner plate with sauce and vegetables spooned over the top.

Makes 4 servings. Per serving: 522 calories, 18 grams fat, 162 milligrams cholesterol and 436 milligrams sodium.

## EAST MEETS WEST - MEETS THE VIRGIN ISLANDS

Virgin Islanders love Chinese cuisine, especially dishes with stir-fried vegetables, sweet and sour sauces, and hot pepper seasonings.

At St. Thomas' *Wok On Water*, Chef/Manager Tam Ho explained that his menu offers items that are from the Hunan, Szechuan, Mandarin and Cantonese regions of China. Hunan cuisine is known for its use of a wide variety of peppers. The Szechuan style of cooking is synonymous with fiery hot peppers and spices. Mandarin and Cantonese dishes are more mild. For those with a timid palate, an asterisk on *Wok On Water's* menu denotes a hot/hot/hot dish.

"The main ingredients we use in cooking are ginger, soy sauce, scallions, hot pepper, and Chinese barbecue sauce," Ho explained. "We slice or shred our meats, fish, and seafood——and chop our vegetables——so they can be easily picked up with chopsticks."

Some of the most common vegetables used in Chinese cooking are bok choy, napa cabbage, straw mushrooms, bamboo shoots, water chestnuts, and baby corn.

*Wok On Water's* Chicken Cashew Nut is a dish that owes its popularity to Virgin Islanders' love of poultry.

## CHICKEN CASHEW NUT

1 16 ounce chicken breast
1/2 egg white
1 tablespoon cornstarch
1 tablespoon soy sauce
2 green peppers, seeded
1 red hot pepper
2/3 cup unsalted cashew nuts
Oil, for deep-fat frying
2 tablespoons oil
15 slices ginger
2 tablespoon soy sauce
1 tablespoon wine
1/2 teaspoon brown vinegar
1 tablespoon cornstarch
1/2 teaspoon salt
1 tablespoon sugar

Cut chicken into bite-sized pieces. Make a marinade from egg white, cornstarch and 1 tablespoon soy sauce. Mix chicken thoroughly with marinade in a mixing bowl. Let stand for at least 30 minutes.

Cut green pepper and red pepper pieces the same size as the chicken. Keep both green pepper and red pepper in separate bowls.

Fry or crisp cashew nuts in the oven. Set aside. Prepare seasoning sauce in a bowl by combining 2 tablespoons soy sauce, wine, brown vinegar, cornstarch, salt and sugar.

Heat oil in a fry pan to 300 to 325 degrees. Deep fry chicken. If the chicken pieces stick to each other, the oil is too hot. Fry for 1/2 minute. Remove chicken and drain.

Remove all but 2 tablespoons oil from fry pan. Quickly stir fry ginger pieces for just a few seconds. Add the green pepper. Add the red pepper now, if you like a hot, spicy dish. Add chicken and seasoning sauce. Stir until thickened and heated thoroughly. Turn off heat and add cashew nuts.

Makes 4 servings. Per serving: 404 calories, 21 grams fat, 83 milligrams cholesterol and 1125 milligrams sodium.

# FISH & SHELLFISH

1. Boiled Fish West Indian Style

2. Fried Native Fish

3. Shrimp Cruzan

4. Herring Gundy

5. Fresh Tuna Marinade

6. Agave Salmon Wellington

7. Blackened Red Snapper

8. Fishermelodie

9. Caribbean Pizza

10. Angel Hair Puttanesca

11. Baked Yellowtail with Spinach & Lobster Stuffing

12. Paella

## THE OCEAN'S BOUNTY

From the days of the Arawak Indians, the inhabitants of the Virgins have relied on the sea's bounty for nourishment. It has been estimated that nearly 500 species of fish inhabit our waters.

Some of the most popular fish are big game species tuna, wahoo and dolphin (also called mahi-mahi, but not the Flipper variety).

Some favorite inshore species of fish in the Virgin Islands include: kingfish, old wife (triggerfish), snapper, grouper, grunt, and hardnose.

Unfortunately, some of these inshore species, especially those which feed around coral reefs, can be carriers of the ciguatera toxin.

This toxin can cause severe illness, even death is extreme cases. Its presence is impossible to detect by looking at the fish. It cannot be seen, felt, smelled, or tasted.

The onset of ciguatera poisoning is often accompanied by nausea, stomach cramps, vomiting, and diarrhea. A tingling in the extremities is another common sign. Many people experience a reversal of temperature sensations: hot feels cold, and cold feels hot.

Bigger, older predator fish (like large barracuda) are more likely to be infected with ciguatera than smaller, deep water fish.

To avoid the risk of ciguatoxin, many restaurants (ironically) purchase their fish from the US mainland. Local residents do well with selecting reef fish under 15 pounds, and knowing their fishermen well. Ciguatoxin is mostly found on the reefs to the south of St. Thomas. North coast reefs have little of this toxin. On St. Croix the problem is far less serious.

Besides fish, other local foods from the sea include queen conch, West Indian top shell or whelk, and spiny or Caribbean lobster.

The first step in preparing an excellent seafood dinner is selecting a good fish.

## ONE FISH, TWO FISH, GOOD FISH, BAD FISH?

Here are seven simple tests you can conduct at the fish market or in the grocery store to help you select a good quality fish.

1. Smell the fish. It should have a fresh, clean, mild "ocean" aroma. Reject any fish that smells excessively "fishy." A strong odor implies that the fish is either old or has been improperly handled.

2. Feel the skin. Good quality fish will have slick, moist skin with scales still firmly attached.

3. Check the fins and tails. Choose fish with moist, flexible fins and tails. Pass by the fish whose fins are dry and ragged.

4. Press the flesh. It should be firm and elastic. When pressing a finger into an aging fish, a visible impression will remain.

5. Examine the eyes. Choose fish whose eyes are clear and full. Reject a fish when its eyes show a lack of moisture and have sunk back into its head.

6. Look at the gills. A fresh fish's gills will vary in color from red to maroon depending on the particular species. A poor quality fish will have traces of grey or brown in its gills.

7. Finally, check the belly. The presence of 'belly burn' or flesh that is pulling away from the bones indicates that the fish has been improperly gutted. There should also be no

breaks or tears in the flesh of a good quality fish.

### EUNICE'S WEST INDIAN RESTAURANT

Tropical fish, like their cold water counterparts, can be prepared in an endless number of ways. One of the unofficial national dishes of the Virgin Islands is boiled fish with a fresh onion butter sauce.

*Eunice's Terrace* in Smith Bay, St. Thomas is one of the best places in the Virgin Islands to try this simple but tasty dish. Eunice serves her Boiled Fish West Indian Style with Fungi, a creamy cornmeal and okra side dish. The recipe for fungi is on page 66.

## BOILED FISH WEST INDIAN STYLE

**4 fish, approx. 1 lb each, scaled and gutted**
**2 medium onions, cut up**
**1 tomato, chopped**
**1 tablespoon vinegar**
**3 tablespoons lemon or lime juice**
**1 teaspoon Accent**
**2 cups water**
**2 teaspoon margarine**
**1 sliced lime for garnish**

Place fish, onions, tomato, vinegar, lemon or lime juice, Accent, water and margarine into a large saucepan. Bring to a boil, then simmer gently for about 20 to 30 minutes, until fish flakes easily when tested with a fork. Serve with sliced lime and fungi.

Makes 4 servings. Per serving: 226 calories, 7 grams fat, 88 milligrams cholesterol and 128 milligrams sodium.

## FRIED NATIVE FISH

The St. John Carnival is celebrated on the Fourth of July. James Dalmida, avid fisherman and well-known cook, has operated a food booth in Carnival Village for several years. With the help of his family, Dalmida serves up generous helpings of Fried Native Fish and Johnny Cakes for hungry celebrants. Here is his recipe:

**4 fish, approx. 1 lb. each, scaled and gutted**
**2 scallions**
**2 sprigs fresh thyme, or 1/4 teaspoon dried**
**1/8 teaspoon ground black pepper**
**1/4 teaspoon salt**
**1/4 cup flour**
**1/4 cup cornmeal**
**oil, for deep-fat frying**
**local hot pepper sauce**

Grind together scallion, thyme, black pepper and salt with a mortar and pestle. Season fish with this mixture. Stir together cornmeal and flour. Coat seasoned fish with this mixture.

Deep fry at 370 degrees for 5 to 8 minutes or until golden brown. Serve with local hot pepper sauce.

Makes 4 servings.

Per serving: 302 calories, 11 grams fat, 88 milligrams cholesterol and 224 milligrams sodium.

## JAN ROBINSON HAS LAUNCHED MANY RECIPES

"While I was chartering, I was always writing down my recipes," said Jan Robinson.

For many years, Robinson worked as both captain and charter chef aboard her 60' steel hull motor-sailer, *Vanity*. During those years, she found that fellow charter yacht chefs also spent hours of time writing down their recipes in an effort to plan exciting gourmet menus for their guests.

"People were always amazed that we could turn out great food from a galley the size of a closet," Robinson said.

So Robinson had the wonderful idea to collect the recipes of her fellow Virgin Islands charter chefs, and assemble them into a cookbook. "I wanted us to be able to share each other's recipes, and also to help make things a little easier for new charter chefs," she said.

Robinson's idea led to not one cookbook, but several: *Ship To Shore I and II, Sip to Shore, Sea to Shore* and most recently, *Sweet to Shore.*

One of her favorite recipes is Shrimp Cruzan, which she often made aboard *Vanity,* and published in *Sea to Shore.*

## SHRIMP CRUZAN

**1 pound large or jumbo shrimp, peeled,**
   **de-veined and butterflied**
**Black pepper**
**Juice of 1 lime**
**4 ounces butter, melted**
**3 ounces cream cheese, softened**
**1 ounce Roquefort or other**
   **blue cheese, softened**
**Paprika and sprigs of parsley, for garnish**

Preheat oven to 400 degrees. Wash shrimp and pat dry. Place in a shallow baking dish. Sprinkle with pepper and lime juice. Blend butter and both cheeses together. Spread over shrimp. Cover with aluminum foil. Bake at 400 degrees for 10 to 15 minutes. Serve over pasta or rice. Sprinkle with paprika and garnish with parsley.

Makes 4 servings. Per serving: 391 calories, 33 grams fat, 240 milligrams cholesterol and 534 milligrams sodium.

# MILDRED V. ANDUZE - A COOK TO REMEMBER

The late Mildred Verona Anduze was truly a remarkable women. She loved to cook, and she enjoyed sharing her knowledge with others. One of her three sons, Dr. Roy Anduze, remembers that in his childhood there was always a kitchen full of young girls who "Mommie" was teaching to cook.

"She loved food," Anduze said, "and she had about 100 god children who she nurtured with both her food and wisdom."

Anduze was just 4 years old when Denmark sold the Virgin Islands to the United States on March 31, 1917. "I'll always remember the tears in my mother's eyes during the transfer ceremony," Anduze said.

Having grown up with much of her girlhood under Danish rule, Mrs. Anduze learned how to prepare many European dishes as well as those native to the Virgin Islands.

For example, salted herring was brought to the islands by the Europeans but it was seasoned into gundy with herbs and spices grown in the islands. (Mrs. Anduze credited her mother, Elizabeth D. Watlington, with developing her culinary talents).

During the 1930's and 1940's, Mrs. Anduze reputation as a fine cook grew. Consequently, she was hired to teach home economics at both the Charlotte Amalie High School and Sts. Peter and Paul.

In this capacity, she served the youth of the island for well over a decade. Dr. Anduze and his wife, Vivian, still have a construction paper booklet with crayon-colored cover containing 16 typed recipes compiled by Mrs. Anduze for the 1948 Charlotte Amalie High School Fair. A wealth of history and knowledge is contained on those (now yellowed) sheets of paper.

By the late 1940's, Mrs. Anduze was locally known as a native gourmet and cook. She made all the young couple's wedding cakes, and was a distinguished personality at the early Carnival Food Fairs, which started in the 1950's.

Dr. Auduze's daughter, Joyce Anduze LaMotta, remembered her grandmother's fine cooking. In 1982, she compiled some of her grandmother's best recipes into the *Mildred V. Anduze Cookbook*. These recipes have surely stood the taste of time!

## HERRING GUNDY

**3 pounds salt herring**
**1-1/2 pounds potatoes, boiled**
**1 large onion**
**2 green peppers, seeded**
**1 hot pepper**
**1/2 cup minced olives**
**1 pint salad oil**
**1/4 cup vinegar**
**1 cup diced beets**
**1/2 cup freshly grated raw carrots**
**Sprig parsley**
**3 hard boiled eggs, chopped**

Rinse herring, remove bones and skin. Put herring, potatoes, onions, pepper, and olives in a meat grinder. Add salad oil and vinegar. Combine thoroughly. Garnish with grated carrots, parsley, hard boiled eggs and diced beets. Usually a little diced beets, a few spoonsful of grated carrots and chopped eggs are stirred into the mixture before garnishing.

Makes 6 servings. Per serving: 561 calories, 44 grams fat, 178 cholesterol and 382 milligrams sodium (*).

* Sodium content of salt herring can vary widely.

## A PASSION FOR COOKING & SPORTFISHING

It's great when you love your profession. But when your profession dovetails perfectly with your favorite hobby, life is almost perfect.

David Wikowski, Food & Beverage Manager at the Sapphire Bay Beach Resort, is such a man. He enjoys cooking almost as much as he does sport fishing. If he's not in the kitchen, he's bobbing over the North Drop attempting to hook a world-record sport fish.

Of course, his love of fishing has allowed him to meet nearly every sportfishing captain in the Virgins— hence a ready supply of 'flopping fresh' fish at Sapphire's *Seagrape Restaurant.*

"There is nothing like the taste of super fresh fish," Wikowski said. "I would rather not have fish on the menu than serve frozen fish."

As well as not serving frozen fish, Wikowski said: "I will never serve an endangered specie like blue marlin or Mako shark."

What fish does he serve? "Something is always in season here—kingfish, dolphin, wahoo, tuna."

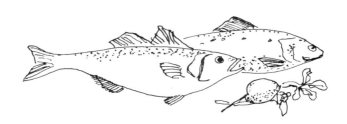

# FRESH TUNA MARINADE

**1 pound very fresh yellowfin tuna, thinly diced, preferably
    from the backbone
Juice from 5 fresh limes
1/2 cup lemon juice
3 tablespoons soy sauce
1/4 cup chopped green onion
1/4 cup chopped onion
Salt and white pepper, to taste
1/2 teaspoon Tabasco sauce
1/2 teaspoon ground ginger
Pinch celery salt**

In a large mixing bowl, combine all of the above ingredients.
Refrigerate for 2 hours and serve chilled.
Makes 4 servings. Per serving: 145 calories, 1 gram fat, 51
milligrams cholesterol and 806 milligrams sodium.

## FRESH FISH AT THE AGAVE TERRACE

Virgin Island visitors and residents alike can enjoy the unique
experience of catching their dinner and having it professionally
prepared—thanks to the *Agave Terrace.*

This restaurant, which is located in the Point Pleasant Resort
close to the sportfishing fleet, has a well-deserved reputation for
having some of the freshest fish in town.

If you want them to cook your just caught catch-of-the day,
it is best to make arrangements as early as possible. They'll
probably ask you to bring your fish in by mid-afternoon.

Later that evening, your fish will be served to you cooked to
perfection.

The *Agave Terrace* always offers a wide range of seafood
dishes, both local and international. They fly fresh seafood in
from the States on a daily basis. Here is a recipe for the

spectacular Agave Salmon Wellington.

# AGAVE SALMON WELLINGTON

**5 ounce salmon fillet**
**1 ounce lobster meat**
**1/4 cup fresh mushrooms**
**1 teaspoon shallots**
**3 tablespoons white wine**
**1 tablespoon butter**
**Puff pastry sheet (5-inch by 5-inch in size)**
**1 egg white**

Finely chop mushrooms and shallots. Saute them in butter and add white wine. Cook until liquid is absorbed, then cool mixture. Add chopped lobster meat to mushroom mixture and place on top of salmon fillet. Then, wrap in puff pastry sheet. Brush with egg wash and bake at 475 degrees Fahrenheit until golden brown.

Makes 1 serving. Per serving: 312 calories, 11 grams fat, 72 milligrams cholesterol and 344 milligrams sodium.

## HINTS ON COOKING FISH

Boiled, baked, stewed, fried, broiled or grilled——fresh fish tastes great. Blackened Red Snapper is basically a simple dish to prepare. However, grilling delicate pieces of fish can sometimes be tricky. Here are five sure-fire tips to assure success.

1. Use a very hot fire. This will seal in the natural juices of the fish.

2. Immediately before placing the fish on the grill, oil the grill to prevent the fish from sticking.

3. Do not move the fish around on the grill. Instead, once placed on the grill, just flip it once during cooking. Excessively moving the fish on the grill could cause it to break apart.

4. Test fish for doneness with your fingertips. When the fish is still raw, it will be soft and springy. Overdone fish is hard and firm. When the fish is done, the flesh will still be soft, but barely firm.

5. Serve freshly grilled fish immediately, on pre-warmed plates.

## BLACKENED RED SNAPPER

**2 tablespoons butter**
**4 fillets red snapper, each**
    **weighing about 6 ounces**
**2 teaspoons finely grated lemon peel**
**1 tablespoon finely minced fresh garlic**
**1 tablespoon fresh chopped**
    **tarragon or 1 teaspoon dried**
**1 tablespoon fresh chopped basil**
    **or 1 teaspoon dried**
**2 teaspoons black pepper**
**1/2 teaspoon cayenne pepper**
**1 tablespoon paprika**
**1/2 teaspoon salt**
**2 fresh lemons or limes, 1 juiced**
    **and 1 cut in wedges to garnish the fish**

Clarify butter by melting it in a small saucepan over low heat. Carefully skim as much of the milky substance off the top of the butter as possible. Tilt pan and spoon out clarified butter, taking care to leave the remaining milky substance on the bottom of the pan.

Wash fish fillets and pat them dry. Lightly coat fish with clarified butter.

Combine lemon peel, garlic, tarragon, basil, black pepper, cayenne pepper, paprika and salt. Rub spice mixture into fish fillets. Place fish in a pan, cover with plastic wrap, place in the refrigerator and allow to sit at least 2 hours or up to 8 hours. This will allow the spices to flavor the flesh of the fish.

When ready to cook, place fish on an oiled grill, skin side down. Cook until spices just begin to blacken, or about 3 to 5 minutes. Turn and moisten the blackened side with lemon or lime juice. Cook other side until just blackened or another 3 to 5 minutes. Serve with wedges of lemon or lime.

Makes 4 servings. Per serving: 146 calories, 7 grams fat, 46 milligrams cholesterol and 379 milligrams sodium.

## SONG OF THE NORTH SEA IN THE VIRGIN ISLANDS

Fishermelodie is a rich seafood stew which blends aspects of both German and Caribbean cuisines into one tasty dish. It is one of the recipes which Petri Dedekind brought to St. Thomas from her home in Bremen, Germany. It is a favorite of customers at her St. Thomas restaurant, the *Windjammer.*

Dedekind said that a bowl of this steaming hot stew was traditionally prepared by wives awaiting their husbands return from commercial fishing trips on the icy North Sea. Her Caribbean version of Fishermelodie is made with tender chunks of dolphin, grouper, or red snapper.

For a recipe from southern Germany, please see page 98.

# FISHERMELODIE

2 strips bacon
1/4 cup onion, diced fine
1/2 green pepper, seeded and diced
2 tomatoes, peeled and chopped
8 ounces tomato juice
1/4 cup white wine
3 cloves minced garlic
Pinch cayenne pepper
2 tablespoons sugar
1/2 onion, sliced into strips
8 1-1/2 ounce pieces fish (dolphin, grouper or snapper)
4 shrimp, peeled and butterflied
8 scallops
6 mussels, canned

Render bacon and mince fine. Add diced onion, green pepper, tomatoes, tomato juice, white wine, garlic, pepper and sugar. Simmer for 5 minutes. Then, add sliced onion and seafood. Poach seafood for 3 to 4 minutes. Serve in a casserole with a crusty loaf of french bread.

Makes 2 servings. Per serving: 343 calories, 5 grams fat, 150 milligrams cholesterol and 882 milligrams sodium.

# PIZZA CARIBBEAN-STYLE

Toussaint Potter is a man of many culinary talents, and baking is one of them. Born in the Virgin Islands, he has been extensively trained abroad.

Today, Potter is the Executive Sous Chef at the *Mangrove Cafe* of the Sugar Bay Resort on St. Thomas.

Although his position requires many skills, he particularly enjoys baking. The menu at the *Mangrove Cafe* includes several specialty pizzas, and Potter makes sure batches of fresh dough are prepared daily. Here is one of his favorite pizza toppings:

**1 8-inch very thin pizza crust**
**5 25/30-count size shrimp, peeled and deveined**
**Cajun spices**
**2 tablespoons olive oil or sesame oil**
**1/4 red onion, sliced thin**
**1/4 red pepper, seeded and diced 1/4 inch  pieces**
**1/4 green pepper, seeded and diced into 1/4 inch pieces**
**3 cloves garlic, pureed to a paste**
**4 ounces grated Parmesan cheese**
**2 tablespoons marinara sauce**

Dip shrimp in Cajun spices and coat evenly. In a skillet, heat the oil very hot and cook shrimp one minute on each side. Remove from pan, cut lengthwise and set aside.

Spread the garlic paste evenly over the dough. Then, spread the marinara sauce the same way. Sprinkle 1/3 of the Parmesan cheese over it. Arrange peppers, onion, shrimp and sprinkle with the rest of the Parmesan. Bake 8 to 10 minutes. Cut into 6 pieces. Makes 2 servings.

Per serving: 404 calories, 25 grams fat, 103 milligrams cholesterol, 1772 sodium.

## MARINARA SAUCE FOR PIZZA

**1/4 teaspoon garlic, minced**
**1 tablespoon olive oil**
**1 tablespoon basil, chopped**
**1 tablespoon oregano, chopped fine**
**1 tablespoon granulated sugar**
**Pinch dry tarragon**
**2-2/3 cups canned whole tomatoes, diced (with juice)**
**6 ounces tomato juice**

In a large saucepan, heat olive oil, add onions first and then add garlic. Saute, but do not brown. Add the tomatoes, juice, spices and sugar. Mix well. Turn heat to very low and let simmer for one hour.

Makes 3 cups sauce. Per two tablespoon serving: 15 calories, 0 fat, 0 cholesterol and 64 milligrams sodium.

### MEDITERRANEAN CUISINE ON ST. CROIX

Dino Dinatale, Chef/Owner of *Dino's* in St. Croix, terms the foods he serves at his restaurant "creative Mediterranean cuisine."

"It's not northern or southern Italian cooking," Dinatale explained, "but more central. I like to use bold flavors like garlic, anchovies, capers, hot peppers, fresh herbs and spices, and four kinds of olives. The essence of Italian food," he concluded, "is fine ingredients, prepared simply."

One of Dinatale's most popular dishes is his Angel Hair Puttanesca . (For recipes from northern and southern Italy, please see pages 123 and 71, respectively).

## ANGEL HAIR PUTTANESCA

**6 ounces capellini pasta**
**6 tablespoons olive oil**
**6 anchovies**
**1 tablespoon chopped garlic**
**2 tablespoons chopped black olives**
**2 tablespoons capers**
**1 tomato, chopped**
**1/2 teaspoon red pepper flakes**
**2 tablespoons chopped fresh basil**

Cook pasta in 2 quarts boiling water.
While pasta is cooking and in a frying pan, warm anchovies

in olive oil for two minutes, breaking up a bit. Add garlic, black olives, capers, tomato, red pepper flakes and fresh basil. Toss two minutes more.

Stir in drained pasta, toss and serve.

Makes 2 servings. Per serving: 519 calories, 44 grams fat, 38 milligrams cholesterol and 489 milligrams sodium.

## ST. JOHN'S CANEEL BAY RESORT

One of the most spectacular features of St. John is its National Park. It comprises almost three-quarters of the island. A stop at the Virgin Islands National Park's Visitor's Center is a must. It is a great way to get oriented to the park's programs and tours.

The foresight to establish a tropical park on St. John came from Laurence Rockefeller in the 1950s. In 1955, Rockefeller also purchased a small resort which sat on the ruins of the old Klein Caneel Plantation. He quickly turned the property into a world renowned hotel, now known as Caneel Bay Resort. (The word "caneel" is the Dutch word for cinnamon).

Today, Caneel Bay Resort continues to be one of the most elegant resorts in the Virgin Islands. It is internationally recognized for its astounding horticulture. There are over 500 species of tropical plants on the property. The Caneel Bay Resort is also known for its first-class cuisine. A buffet at Caneel Bay is a real treat. A whole roast suckling pig, fresh tropical salads, lush fruits, and desserts 'to-die-for' are everyday menu items.

Chef David Bowman has created a very special seafood entree he calls,"Baked Yellowtail With Spinach and Lobster Stuffing." Here is his recipe.

# BAKED STUFFED YELLOWTAIL

**1 clove garlic, chopped**
**2 shallots, chopped**
**2 ounces butter**
**1 6-ounce bag fresh chopped spinach**
**1 ounce Pernod**
**8 ounces cooked lobster meat**
**Salt and pepper, to taste**
**1-1/2 to 2 pound yellowtail filet**

In a fry pan, saute the garlic and shallots in butter for a few minutes. Add the chopped spinach. Saute for two more minutes. Add the Pernod, lobster meat, salt and pepper to taste.

Lay out the fillet on a flat surface. Season lightly with salt and pepper. Cover the fillet with the stuffing and roll. Bake in a 450 degree oven for 15 minutes.

Makes 4 servings. Per serving: 253 calories, 13 grams fat, 123 milligrams cholesterol and 437 milligrams sodium.

## DELICIOUS SPANISH IMPORTS

Christopher Columbus brought the first Spaniards to the Caribbean, and their culinary influence is still being felt. Jose Lavilla, manager of *Acacia* at the Yacht Haven Marina on St. Thomas, describes the dishes they serve from the Catalan region of Spain as: "down-to-earth cooking which is basic and natural."

In this southern region of Spain, dishes which contain shrimp, clams, scallops, squid, octopus, snails and sea urchin are popular. The use of such a diverse supply of seafood is evident in the restaurant's large tapas menu. Tapas are small servings or 'tastes' of savory dishes. It is common to order four to six tapas for a couple to share as a meal. "People like to eat a variety of foods, and that is why tapas have such a long tradition," Lavilla explained.

Another popular dish—Lavilla called it the unofficial national dish of Spain—is a seafood studded, flavorful rice dish called Paella. Here is *Acacia's* recipe:

# PAELLA - *ACACIA* STYLE

**Olive oil**
**1/2 pound squid**
**1/2 pound chicken pieces**
**4 cups rice**
**6 garlic cloves, chopped**
**1 small onion, chopped**
**1 green pepper, seeded & chopped**

**Fish Stock (\*)**

**Saffron**
**12 clams**
**Salt & Black pepper**
**8 shrimp**
**12 mussels**
**1/2 cup green peas**
**1 red pepper**
**1 fresh lemon**

In a large paella pan - (a large, flat stainless steel or cast iron skillet, or clay casserole can be substituted for this special piece of cookware) - pour the olive oil and fry the chicken pieces, garlic, onion, green pepper and squid. When chicken and squid are done and vegetables are tender, add rice. Continue frying mixture, stirring constantly, for a few minutes.

Add 2-1/2 cups fish stock (\* see below) for each cup of rice and bring mixture to a boil. Simmer for a few minutes. Taste mixture, then add saffron, salt and pepper to taste, as needed.

Place mixture in a pre-heated 350 degree oven. Bake for approximately 20 minutes, or until rice has absorbed all the liquid and is dry. Do not over cook the rice.

About five minutes before rice is done, place the shrimp, clams, mussels and peas, decoratively over the top.

Oil the red pepper and place it in the oven for a few minutes to roast. Then peel, slice and also place on top of paella.

Finally, decorate the top with wedges of fresh lemon before serving.

Makes 4 full-meal sized servings. Per serving: 794 calories, 13 grams fat, 490 milligrams cholesterol and 1191 milligrams sodium.

## (*) FISH STOCK

To make fish stock at home, place foods such as leftover heads of fish, fish bones, chicken bones, head or shells of lobster, and any other fish trimmings into a large pot with water. Bring to a boil. Lower heat and simmer for 2 to 3 hours. When cool, strain and refrigerate liquid.

When making this paella recipe, you can opt to pre-cook shrimp, squid, clams and mussels in stock. As soon as shrimp and squid are done (in 3 to 4 minutes) and clams and mussels have just opened, remove them to a separate platter. Simmer the rest of the stock for 2 to 3 hours and add salt and pepper to taste.

## SWEETS

1. Gooseberries on a Stick

2. Tie Tie Sugar Cake

3. Shingle Cake

4. Dundersloe

5. Jawbone

6. Red Grout

7. Soursop Ice Cream

8. Crown Cantaloupe with Banana Flambe

9. Key Lime Pie

10. Gertrude Melchior's Wedding Cake

11. Mocko Jumbie

12. Coconut Tart

13. Pineapple Tart

14. Guava Tart

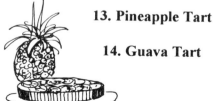

## OLD FASHIONED SWEETNESS

Enid Leonard fondly remembers how wonderful food tasted "back in the good old days." She still enjoys keeping the old cooking traditions alive. Today she regularly makes old fashioned candies like stewed-gooseberries-on-a-stick and tie-tie-sugar-cakes.

When it comes time to shape her ginger and cinnamon sprinkled shingle cakes into small rectangles, modern cookie cutters just won't do for Leonard. She cuts each by hand. (The tiny cross-hatch cuts she marks in the dough make these sweets resemble roof-top shingles, hence the name.)

The method for making these goodies go back several generations in her family.

"I learned to cook from my grandmother," Leonard said. "Every Saturday, she would go down to the market with the other ladies. It was there that she would sell her trays of coconut sugar cakes, dundersloe, peppermint candies, royal cake, shingle cake, double deck, jaw bones, gooseberries-on-a-stick, and all kinds of tarts."

Here are Leonard's three special recipes for old-time Virgin Island sweets:

## STEWED GOOSEBERRIES ON A STICK

**4 cups gooseberries**
**Water**
**1 to 1-1/2 pounds sugar**
**A few cinnamon sticks**

Remove the tiny stems from gooseberries. Prick each berry two to three times, to remove acid. Soak berries in water overnight. The next morning, drain berries. Place berries in a large saucepan or kettle and add fresh water enough to cover. Add sugar and cinnamon sticks. Bring to a boil, reduce heat and simmer, stirring occasionally, until berries turn brown - about 2 hours.

From a coconut palm, trim a frond into small sticks or purchase wooden skewers from the grocery. Push gooseberries down onto skewers. Stewed gooseberries can also be served in a little paper cup.

Some of the leftover gooseberry syrup can be made into a beverage by adding a little extra water, sugar and spices.

Makes 12 sticks of gooseberries. Per stick: 164 calories, 0 milligrams fat, 0 milligrams cholesterol and 0 milligrams sodium.

## TIE TIE SUGAR CAKE

**1 tablespoon crushed fresh ginger**
**2 cups water**
**2 tablespoons dried orange peel**
**1 cup brown sugar**
**1 coconut**

Make a syrup out of ginger, water, orange peel and brown sugar. Grate coconut meat. Stir grated coconut meat into syrup. Boil, stirring occasionally to prevent burning, for about an hour or until syrup is a honey-like consistency.

Take pieces of coconut shell. Remove husk and wash shell. Put to dry. When dry, fill pieces of coconut shell with tie tie sugar cakes. Cover with plastic wrap.

Makes approximately 12 pieces. Per piece: 116 calories, 4 grams fat, 0 milligrams cholesterol and 8 milligrams sodium.

# SHINGLE (OR LONG) CAKE

1/3 cup shortening, melted
3/4 cup light molasses
1/4 to 1/2 cup brown sugar
3 cups flour
1/2 teaspoon salt
2 teaspoons ginger
1 teaspoon baking soda
1 teaspoon cinnamon

Place shortening, molasses and brown sugar in a saucepan. Melt by bringing ingredients to a boil, then cool immediately.

Sift flour, salt, ginger, baking soda and cinnamon. Add liquid ingredients to dry. Mix well. Roll out dough on a floured board and cut into "shingles" about 8-inches long and 3-inches wide. Cut slits in the long dough pieces to resemble shingles. Bake on a greased cookie sheet at 350 degrees Fahrenheit for 10 to 15 minutes.

Makes approximately 12 shingles. Per shingle: 237 calories, 6 grams fat, 0 milligrams cholesterol and 163 milligrams sodium.

## GOOD FOOD - LUCIA HENLEY STYLE

On St. Thomas and St. John, when you think of a mouth-watering display of baked goods, candies, and preserves——you think of Lucia Henley. This talented island cook has won many awards at local food fairs for her delicious and beautifully presented foods.

Henley credits her mother, Daisy Testamark——who was a native of St. John and professional chef——for her culinary education. In turn, Henley is deeply concerned that today's young people are not learning about traditional foods. "Ask a child what dundersloe or jawbone are and they probably can't tell you," she said.

In addition to working full time (in a non-cooking field), Henley has often used her spare time to teach local children about the islands' native foods. "I enjoy passing down some of what I know," she said.

Dundersloe is an old time candy that Henley enjoys making and it is a food that captured her imagination as a child. "It was so amazing to see peanuts in glass," Henley said, about the appearance of peanuts hardened in a shiny sugar solution.

Red and white Jawbone is another favorite old time candy which Henley finds especially fun to make with young people.

Here are her recipes:

## DUNDERSLOE

**2-1/3 cups granulated sugar**
**1 cup water**
**1 pound shelled, unsalted peanuts**

Combine sugar and water in a saucepan. Heat to 310 degrees Fahrenheit, until mixture is light brown in color.

In a non-stick coated or oiled muffin tin, place unsalted peanuts, filling about half full. Pour sugar mixture into each muffin tin over peanuts, until muffin tins are filled. Cool on kitchen counter. When cool, invert to remove individual dundersloe. If there is a problem removing dundersloe from muffin tins, run a little hot water over the bottom of the tins and dundersloe should pop out.

Makes about 12 dundersloe. Per dundersloe: 387 calories, 9 grams fat, 0 milligrams cholesterol and 3 milligrams sodium.

## JAWBONE

**4-3/3 cups sugar, divided into two 2-1/3 portions**
**2 cups water, divided into two 1 cup portions**
**1/4 to 1/2 teaspoon oil of peppermint**
**a few drops red food coloring**

In a large saucepan, combine 2-1/3 cups sugar and 1 cup water. Cover pan and slowly heat until mixture reaches between 310 and 325 degrees Fahrenheit. When sufficiently hot, pour mixture onto an oiled marble stone. Make an indentation into the mixture using a finger or spoon. Pour in the oil of peppermint. With hands, a knife or scraper, pick up ends and fold into the middle of the mixture. Continue this process of folding until the mixtures becomes firm and begins to hold its shape.

Meanwhile, pound a clean nail into a board and stand the board upright. Oil the nail. Lift the hot sugar mixture and hang it from the nail. As it stretches, fold the mixture up, continually repeating until mixture turns brownish white in color. As it cools and hardens a bit, begin to pull off lengths about 7 to 8 inches long and place them on waxed paper.

Then, combine the second half of the sugar and 1 cup water in a saucepan and heat to 310 to 325 degrees Fahrenheit. Turn heat off, add red food coloring to mixture. Pour this red sugar mixture on oiled marble stone and work as above until it becomes firm. After hanging mixture on nail, pull off pieces and wrap them in candy cane fashion around the white sticks of cooked sugar. Cool.

Makes about 12 jawbone. Per jawbone: 284 calories, 0 grams fat, 0 milligrams cholesterol and 0 milligrams sodium.

## THE DANISH AND WEST INDIAN COMBINED

In the Virgin Islands, Transfer Day (March 31) celebrates the United States purchasing St. Thomas, St. Croix and St. John from Denmark in 1917. (Just imagine waking up as a Dane, and going to sleep as an American!)

The foods traditionally used to celebrate this island-wide holiday are, of course, a combination of European and Caribbean flavors.

"The Danes traditionally used to make their 'Rodgrod' or Red Grout with strawberries and raspberries," explained St. Croix native Jennie Lawaetz. "But here in the Caribbean, they used guavas and prickly pear juice to make the red coloring."

Lawaetz learned much about cooking from her father, Frederick Christensen. But it was her best friend, Amy MacKay, who taught her how to cook Red Grout. (Amy MacKay is the author of the delightful cookbook entitled, "Le Awe Cook", which translates to "Let Us Cook.")

Here's the recipe:

## "RODGROD" OR RED GROUT

**2 ripe prickly pear fruit or 1/8 tsp red food coloring**
**1 quart water**
**8 firm ripe guavas**
**1/2 cup sugar, optional**
**1 cup quick-cooking tapioca**
**1/2 cup raisins**
**1/2 cup pitted prunes, chopped**
**Pinch salt**
**Milk or cream**

Prepare prickly pears by rubbing off their spines, butting them open and placing them in a pan. Pour one cup of boiling water over the fruit. Steep for several minutes. Strain off and save all the liquid from the fruit to color the dish later.

Remove stems from the guavas and cut them into pieces. Boil for 10 minutes with enough water to cover. Add sugar if desired. Remove from heat and strain liquid. Discard the pulp and seeds.

Return pot to low heat and add tapioca, stirring vigorously to prevent lumping. Continue to cook until grains are crystal clear. Add raisins, chopped prunes and salt. Stir well and cook for 5 minutes longer. Add coloring last. Pour mixture into mold and chill. Serve with milk or cream.

Makes 6 servings. Per serving (with one tablespoon cream): 240 calories, 6 grams fat, 20 milligrams cholesterol and 81 milligrams sodium.

## SOURSOP MAKES A SWEET DESSERT

Like the mango and papaya, the soursop is a common Caribbean fruit. Soursops can grow to be quite large, reaching to 8 inches in length. They can weight up to 6 pounds. Individual fruit are oval-shaped with a dark green spiny skin. The soursop's skin remains green when ripe, but the flesh softens to the touch. Underneath the green skin, the soursop's flesh is white, often with a pink tint. When the flesh has been sieved through a strainer and seeds removed, the resulting juice has the consistency of a thick pudding.

A one pound soursop provides 161 calories. It is a good source of Vitamin C, dietary fiber, and iron.

Although soursop can be eaten in many ways, most commonly it is used as a beverage or as a flavoring in ice cream.

# SOURSOP ICE CREAM

1 cup half & half cream
1/3 cup sugar
1 tablespoon cornstarch
Pinch salt
1 teaspoon vanilla or almond essence
2 egg whites
1 cup heavy whipping cream
1 medium-sized ripe soursop

Scald the half & half in the top of a double boiler. Combine the sugar, cornstarch and salt. Stir in enough scalded half & half so that the mixture can be poured. Add this mixture to remaining half & half in the top of the double boiler. Stir half & half, cornstarch and salt until thickened, then cover and cook for 10 minutes over low heat. Cool and add essence.

Beat egg whites until stiff. In a second bowl, whip the heavy cream. Fold the cooled cornstarch mixture and whipped cream into the egg whites.

Peel the soursop. Mash the pulp through a sieve and press out all the liquid. Add liquid to the prepared cream mixture and stir well. Place the soursop flavored mixture into a shallow square pan or ice cube trays. Place in the freezer. When the ice cream has begun to freeze around the edges of the tray, take it out of the freezer. Turn it into a bowl and beat it with an electric mixer until smooth and no frozen chunks remain. This will reduce the size of the crystals in the final product and produce a smoother ice cream.

Return mixture to the trays and freeze until firm.

Ice cream can be eaten immediately or kept frozen for several weeks.

Makes 4 cups. Per one-half cup serving: 215 calories, 14 grams fat, 52 milligrams cholesterol and 85 milligrams sodium.

## WONDERFUL WENDELL WALKER

Wendell Walker has had an exciting career as a master chef. He first entered a professional kitchen while still a teenager. He worked as a cook's helper to a master French chef at a hotel on his home island of Barbuda.

After moving to St. Thomas in the mid-1960's, Walker spent the next decade steadily advancing through ranks of his choosen profession. He worked for *Bluebeard's Castle*, and eventually became the Executive Chef at *Frenchmen's Reef*.

During these years, Walker furthered his culinary education by taking courses at such prestigious places as the *Greenbriar Hotel* in West Virginia and the *Hyatt Regency* in Atlanta.

Walker briefly opened his own restaurant on St. Thomas, but soon left to pursue another challenge. He landed a job as the Executive Sous Chef at *Biltmore Hotel* in California. It was an exciting opportunity, and he cooked for movie stars on a daily basis. He even catered the movie 'Beverly Hills Cop'.

Today, Walker is once again back on St. Thomas. His most recent position has been Executive Chef (and co-owner) of the *Sunset View Restaurant* at *Bluebeard's Castle*.

Here is one of the magnificent desserts he prepares for his guests:

## CANTALOUPE WITH BANANA FLAMBE

**2 ounces butter**
**1/4 pound sugar**
**6 ounces concentrated orange juice**
**1 ounce Grand Marnier**
**1 ounce Cointreau**
**3 bananas, sliced**
**3 cantaloupes**
**Ice cream**

Combine butter and sugar in a frying pan, occasionally stirring until lightly browned. Add orange juice and liquor. Simmer before adding sliced bananas. This makes the banana flambe mixture.

Cut cantaloupes in crown style. Remove seeds, add ice cream of your choice. Flambe bananas and pour over ice cream.

Makes 6 servings. Per serving: 365 calories, 11 grams fat, 40 milligrams cholesterol and 105 milligrams sodium.

## CHIEF CHEF ON CRUISE SHIPS

Charlotte Amalie Harbor just would not be the same without four or five cruise ships tied to its docks. Each week, passenger ships of all sizes enter St. Thomas. Each is a microcosm of luxury, entertainment, and good food.

For the Royal Caribbean Cruise Line (whose ships include *Sovereign of the Seas, Monarch of the Seas* and *Majesty of the Seas*), there is a single man who is ultimately in charge of all the meals. His name is Emil W. Graf. He decides what the menu will be, exactly how it will be prepared, and how it will be served.

As the corporate director of food operations for the cruise line, Graf has planned his week-long menu to feature a different ethnic cuisine each evening. For Caribbean night, he features a classic favorite——Key Lime Pie——for dessert.

## KEY LIME PIE

**2 14-ounce cans sweetened condensed milk**
**2 egg yolks**
**3/4 cups fresh lime juice**
**1/2 cup whipping cream**
**1 9-inch pre-baked pie shell**

Combine condensed milk and beaten egg yolks. Gradually

add lime juice. Fill pie shell with the mixture. Bake in a 350 degree Fahrenheit oven for 8 to 10 minutes. Do not allow to brown. Chill in the refrigerator for two hours or more.

Whip the cream and garnish with a rosette of the whipped cream before serving.

Makes 8 servings. Per serving: 461 calories, 18 grams fat, 90 milligrams cholesterol and 270 milligrams sodium.

## YOU NEED A TALL APPETITE FOR THIS DESSERT

In the early 1990's, Executive Chef Sarah Bowman of the *Stouffer Grand Beach Resort* wanted to create a special, unique dessert for their *Baywind Restaurant*. They asked their hotel patrons, their friends, and even the proverbial 'man on the street' to name their favorite dessert. The overwhelmingly answer was strawberry shortcake.

Since they wanted to create this special tropical dessert using island foods, they decided to use a thick, rich local bread called dumb bread—but to form the dough into small biscuits instead of the traditional large round loaf. Then, they chose an assortment of Caribbean fruits for the topping.

Since the dessert was piled sky high, they decided to name it 'Mocko Jumbie' after the festive silt dancers of carnival.

# THE BAYWIND'S MOCKO JUMBIE

1 tablespoon sugar
1/4 cup shortening
l egg
1/4 cup milk
2 cups all-purpose flour
l/2 teaspoon salt
1 teaspoon baking powder
1/4 cup coconut
l small orange
l/2 small ripe papaya
l small ripe mango
l small ripe banana
l guava
l kiwi
l/2 cup sugar
l/2 cup water
2 tablespoons Virgin Islands rum
l orange, cut into slices
l lemon, cut into slices
Whipped Cream, for garnish
Confectioner's sugar, for garnish

To make the dumb bread: Cream together sugar and shortening. Add egg, then scrape bowl. Continue to mix on low speed. Slowly add milk and scrape bowl. In a separate bowl, combine flour, salt, baking powder and coconut. Add dry ingredients to liquid and mix until smooth. On a floured surface, roll dough approximately 1/2 inch thick. Let rest for 10 to 15 minutes. Cut out biscuit rounds 3 inches in diameter. Place on a sheet pan and bake at 375 degrees for 10 to 15 minutes, or until lightly browned. Let cool.

Peel all fruit and cut into bite-size pieces. Sprinkle fruit with sugar and a little rum, to taste. Let fruit marinate for 10 to 15 minutes.

Make a simple rum-flavored sugar syrup by combining sugar, water, orange and lemon slices in a saucepan. Bring ingredients to a boil, then let simmer for 10 to 15 minutes. Add two tablespoons rum and let cool.

Slice dumb bread biscuits in half and soak with rum-flavored sugar syrup. This can be done by either spooning syrup onto biscuits for placing syrup in a pie dish and pressing cut biscuit halves into the syrup to coat.

To assemble: Generously place marinated fruit on top of the bottom half of a biscuit. Then, top fruit with whipped cream and set the other half of the biscuit on top, slightly off to the side. Sprinkle top of biscuit with confectioner's sugar.

Makes 10 servings. Per serving: 280 calories, 9 grams fat, 20 milligrams cholesterol, 164 milligrams sodium.

## A WEDDING CAKE - VIRGIN ISLANDS STYLE

"When my husband can't find me," said well-known St. Thomas native, Gertrude Melchior, "he knows to look in the kitchen."

In her kitchen, Melchior's love of baking is readily apparent. Several round pans, some as large as 18 inches wide, sit in a corner. Books on cake decorating lay open on the counter. Her kitchen is obviously a well-used, much loved place.

Melchior says that she especially enjoys baking traditional black wedding cakes.

She credits her mother, Ingebord Petersen Lockhart, for being her culinary inspiration.

"Mother always made Christmas special," reports Melchior.

Lockhart would bake luscious sweetbreads in small tin coffee cans as gifts. Recipients received not only the sweet bread, but also a picnic ham and some material for kitchen curtains. Melchior remembers Christmas Eve as a wonderfully busy day as she helped her mother deliver all the goodies.

Christmas Day was always a family day, and this is still true for Melchior today. For the last several years, she has hosted the family meal at her home.

Her menu includes a roast suckling pig, traditional stuffed turkey, and a clove-adorned ham. This is in addition to her spicy potato stuffing, candied fruits, Danish-style asparagus pudding, croustades, dumb bread, and, of course, sweet bread for dessert.

The following is Melchior's recipe for Wedding Cake. On page 73 is her recipe for Asparagus Pudding and on page 125 is her recipe for Croustades Filled with Creamed Chicken.

## GERTRUDE MELCHIOR'S WEDDING CAKE

**4 boxes raisins, 2 seeded and 2 seedless**
**2 pounds currants**
**2 pounds cut mixed dried fruit**
**2 pounds prunes**
**1/4 pound sweet almonds**
**4 tablespoons cinnamon**
**1 tablespoon mace**
**1 tablespoon nutmeg**
**1 tablespoon allspice**
**1 bottle brandy**
**1 bottle blackberry liqueur**
**1 bottle Cherry Herring**
**1 pint molasses**
**1 pound brown sugar**
**1-1/2 pounds butter**
**1 pound sugar**
**2 teaspoons baking soda**
**2 pounds flour**
**2 teaspoons salt**
**10 eggs**

Grind fruits and almonds. Soak with spices, brandy, blackberry liqueur, 1/2 bottle Cherry Herring, molasses and brown sugar.

Cream butter and sugar until light and fluffy. Sift together flour, baking soda and salt. Beat eggs until they turn a lemon yellow. Then add to butter and sugar mixture, alternating with flour mixture, while stirring constantly. After cake batter is well mixed, add fruits and stir well.

Bake in well-greased pans in a 350 degree oven until done. When done, pour the remaining half bottle of Cherry Herring over the cake and let it soak.

Makes approximately 72 slices. Per slice: 434 calories, 9 grams fat, 21 milligrams cholesterol and 185 milligrams sodium.

# TROPICAL TARTS

Aloha Morales has been making tarts since she was a young girl. "On Saturdays, my sister and I would visit her godmother," Morales explained. "First, we were only allowed to watch as she made her special tarts, but after awhile she allowed us to help."

Morales makes her tarts with such popular fillings as grated coconut, crushed pineapple, or stewed guava. She makes common size tarts (8 or 9 inches), as well as smaller ones. She also learned how to weave the strips of dough in lattice fashion to decorate the tops of the tarts.

## BASIC TART CRUST:

4 tablespoons butter
4 tablespoons shortening
1/4 cup sugar
5 tablespoons milk
1 egg
1 tablespoon baking powder
1 teaspoon vanilla essence
1 teaspoon almond essence
1-1/2 cups flour

In a mixing bowl, combine butter and shortening. Cream in sugar, using an electric mixer. Blend in milk, egg, baking powder and vanilla and almond essence.

By hand, stir in 1 cup flour. With fingers, work in an additional 1/2 cup flour to make a stiff dough.

Place dough on a floured surface and roll until 1/8 inch thick. Cut dough to fit a 9 inch pie pan or 6 smaller circles to fit into muffin tins. Save some dough to cut into strips to make a lattice shape decoration on top.

Makes enough dough for shell for 1 large tart or 6 muffin-size tarts.

To assemble tart, spoon filling into tart shell(s). Add enough filling to equal 1/4 inch thick for a large pie or about 2 tablespoons each for small muffin size tarts. Crimp dough around outside of tart and place strips of dough in crisscross fashion over top of filling.

Bake in a 375 degree oven for approximately 15 to 20 minutes, or until bubbly and brown.

Makes 6 servings. Per serving (shell only): 309 calories, 17 grams fat, 56 milligrams cholesterol, and 26 milligrams sodium.

## COCONUT FILLING

**1 cup freshly grated coconut**
**3/4 cup sugar**
**1/4 cup water**
**1/4 teaspoon vanilla essence**

In a saucepan over medium-high heat, combine grated coconut, sugar, water. Simmer, stirring occasionally so that sugar does not burn, for about 40 minutes. Add vanilla essence when filling is almost done. Mixture is done when it loses its milky white appearance and turns clear and glassy.

Makes enough to fill 1 large tart or 6 muffin size.

Per serving(not including shell): 138 calories, 4 grams fat, 0 milligrams cholesterol and 3 milligrams sodium.

## PINEAPPLE FILLING

**1-1/2 cups fresh pineapple chopped fine**
**1/2 cup sugar**
**1/4 teaspoon ground cinnamon**

Combine pineapple and sugar in a saucepan and simmer over medium-high heat, stirring occasionally, for about 30 minutes. Add cinnamon just before done. Filling should thicken when done. Makes 1 large tart or 6 muffin size. Per serving (not including shell): 79 calories, 0 grams fat, 0 milligrams cholesterol and 0 milligrams sodium.

## GUAVA FILLING

**3 to 4 fresh guavas (about 1 pound)**
**3/4 cup sugar**
**2 tablespoons water**
**1/4 teaspoon vanilla essence**

Wash guavas, cut in half and remove seeds. In a saucepan, combine guavas, sugar and water. Simmer over medium-high heat, stirring occasionally for about 30 to 40 minutes, or until filling thickens. Just before done, add vanilla essence.

Makes enough to fill 1 large tart or 6 of the muffin size.

Per serving (not including shell): 121 calories, 0 grams fat, 0 milligrams cholesterol and 1 milligram sodium.

# EXTRAS

**1. Papaya Jam**

**2. Mango Chutney**

**3. Basil Pesto**

**4. Herb Butter**

**5. Herb Mayonnaise**

**6. Herb Vinegar**

**7. Hot Pepper Sauce**

## EXTRAS

Call them 'extras' or 'condiments' or what ever you like. The recipes that follow add spice, zip and zing to foods.

## CHERYL'S FAVORITES

Cheryl Miller is a very multi-talented lady. Originally from New York, she has now lived on St. John for nearly twenty years. During that time, she has worked at a wide variety of jobs ranging from artist to social worker. But it is Miller's latest venture which uses her diverse talents so deliciously.

The humble beginnings of *A Taste of Paradise* started when Miller sold a batch of her home-made spicy mustard at a local arts and crafts fair.

She received so many compliments (and additional orders) that she decided to go into business. At first she operated out of her home kitchen, but soon outgrew such a limited space. Her bustling wholesale food company is currently located in the St. John Lumber Building Complex.

She now offers a complete line of specialty foods which include tropical jellies, jams, chutney, hot sauces, and pesto.

While some commercial products *claim* to capture the individual taste of a particular locale, Miller's actually do. This because many of her ingredients are locally grown.

In her backyard, Miller has a passion fruit vine, a tamarind, and a papaya tree. Her aunt in Coral Bay has mango and guava trees, and grows fresh basil and sweet spinach in her tiny garden. Miller uses these ingredients to make passion fruit jelly, tamarind jelly, guava jelly, papaya jam, mango chutney, and basil pesto. Of course, she also continues to make her famous Sweet, Hot and Spicy Mustard. Miller sells her products at many stores throughout the Virgin Islands.

# CHERYL'S FAVORITE PAPAW JAM

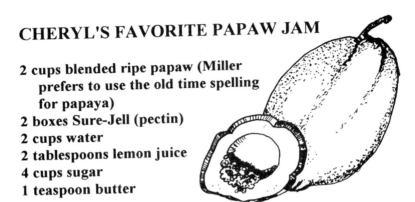

2 cups blended ripe papaw (Miller
     prefers to use the old time spelling
     for papaya)
2 boxes Sure-Jell (pectin)
2 cups water
2 tablespoons lemon juice
4 cups sugar
1 teaspoon butter

In a 6 to 8 quart saucepan, place the papaw, Sure-Jell, water and lemon juice. Bring to a boil, and let boil for 2 to 3 minutes, stirring occasionally. Miller recommends using a wooden spoon for stirring jam ingredients. Add the sugar and bring to a hard, rolling boil for 3 to 4 minutes. To reduce the frothy `skim' that rises to the top, Miller recommends adding a teaspoon of butter.

Miller said that she can tell when her jam has boiled to the correct consistency by counting the drops as the jam rolls off her wooden spoon. When only 8 drops fall and the rest of the jam gels on the spoon as she removes it from the boiling mixture, it is ready. At this point, Miller suggests using a clean metal spoon to remove any remaining `skim'. Then, pour jam into heat sterilized jars and cap. Place jars into water and boil 1-1/2 minutes to seal. Remove to a towel, dry and label.

Makes approximately 6 cups of jam. Per 2 tablespoon serving: 63 calories, 0 grams fat, 0 milligrams cholesterol and 1 milligram sodium.

# MANGO CHUTNEY

10 large ripe mangoes
1 cup raisins
1 cup vinegar
1 cup lime juice
1-1/2 cups sugar (can use brown sugar, but the chutney will
    be darker in color)
1 chili pepper or 1/2 tsp dried chili pepper
1 garlic bulb
1 onion
1 tablespoon mustard seed
1 tablespoon celery seed
1-1/2 tablespoon salt
1 freshly ground knob of ginger
1/4 teaspoon ground cloves

Mix all ingredients together. Set overnight on kitchen counter. The next day, simmer ingredients for 3 hours, stirring occasionally. Pour into sterilized jars and cap. Place jars back into water and boil 1-1/2 minutes to seal. Remove to a towel, dry and label.

Makes approximately 10 cups. Per 2 tablespoon serving: 38 calories, 0 grams fat, 0 milligrams cholesterol and 121 milligrams sodium.

# BASIL PESTO

1 cup olive oil
1/2 cup fresh basil
1/2 cup sweet spinach (or you can use parsley)
1/2 cup grated Parmesan cheese
2 to 3 pine nuts
2 cloves garlic
Large pinch salt, small pinch pepper

Blend basil, sweet spinach or parsley and 1/2 cup of the olive oil. Add the rest of the oil, Parmesan cheese, pine nuts, garlic, salt and pepper. Put blended ingredients in clean jars. Keep refrigerated.

Makes approximately 2-1/2 cups. Per 2 tablespoon serving: 109 calories, 12 grams fat, 2 milligrams cholesterol and 75 milligrams sodium.

## FRESH HERBS - FLAVOR WITHOUT THE SALT

Every Saturday morning at Charlotte Amalie's Market Square, local vendors sell all types of garden fresh foods. Their herbs and spices are especially tasty. Fresh thyme and basil are available all year. After a good rain, rosemary and marjoram can be found.

Thyme, basil, rosemary and marjoram——like other fresh herbs——work by enhancing the natural flavors in food. While they add flavor, they do not add sodium or calories. They also contain important nutrients like Vitamin A, and minerals like iron, magnesium and zinc.

Here are a few popular ways that these fresh herbs are used:

**THYME:** Because of its aromatic nature, thyme is usually used sparingly as a background flavor. Paired with a bay leaf, it is excellent in meat, poultry and fish stews. Tie together six to eight stalks of fresh thyme to boil in broths and soups. Use the leaves alone to season meats, soups, stews and stuffings. Fresh thyme is an essential ingredient in native seasoning mixes for poultry and red meats.

**BASIL:** This delicate, fragrant herb is often used in tomato dishes. Chopped fresh basil also enhances cold salads. It also goes well with potato, cucumber or seafood. To make an attractive garnish, sprinkle sliced cherry tomato halves with finely chopped fresh basil.

**ROSEMARY:** One of the more fragrant herbs, rosemary is used with lamb and pork. Fresh chopped rosemary leaves also add a wonderful flavor to bread-based poultry stuffings. Another interesting combination is freshly chopped rosemary over sliced orange sections.

**MARJORAM:** This herb has a sweet, tangy taste that adds substance to meat pies. It also enhances soups, sauces, stuffings, and stews.

Fresh herbs also can be used to make other 'extras' or 'condiments' like seasoned butters, mayonnaise and vinegar. Here's how:

## FRESH HERB BUTTER

**1 cup butter (or margarine, if you like)**
**1/3 cup chopped fresh herbs (see list of herbs, above)**
**2 teaspoons lemon juice (lime juice is better, if using**
**fresh herb butter for fish)**

Combine all ingredients in a blender or food processor and whirl until well mixed. Cover and refrigerate overnight. Can be used for up to two weeks.

Makes 1-1/2 cups whipped herb butter. Per one tablespoon serving (made with butter): 101 calories, 11 grams fat, 31 milligrams cholesterol and 117 milligrams sodium. Per one tablespoon serving (made with margarine): 102 calories, 11 grams fat, 0 milligrams cholesterol and 133 milligrams sodium.

## FRESH HERB MAYONNAISE

**1 cup mayonnaise**
**1/2 cup fresh chopped herbs (see list of herbs, above)**
**2 teaspoons lemon juice**

Combine all ingredients in a mixing bowl. Cover and refrigerate overnight to blend flavors. Remains good for up to 4 weeks.

Makes 1-1/4 cup. Per one tablespoon serving: 100 calories, 11 grams fat, 8 milligrams cholesterol and 79 milligrams sodium.

## FRESH HERB VINEGAR

**1 cup white wine vinegar**
**1/4 cup chopped fresh green herbs (see list of herbs, above)**
**1 clove garlic**

Combine all ingredients in a glass jar. Cover the jar with plastic wrap and store unrefrigerated for about 3 weeks. When ready to use, strain liquid through a fine mesh strainer or cheesecloth and transfer liquid to another jar. Herb vinegar will remain good for several months.

Makes 1 cup. Per one tablespoon serving: 1 calorie, 0 grams fat, 0 milligrams cholesterol and 1 milligram sodium.

### HERE'S HOW TO DRY FRESH HERBS AT HOME

1. Wash herbs, pat dry and strip leaves from stems, flowers and/or seeds.

2. Place herbs on a large baking sheet.

3. Put herb filled baking sheet out in the sun to dry or dry in

an oven. (Beware! Oven temperatures of more than 200 degrees can cause herbs to lose their flavor.)

4. Test herbs for dryness in two to three days by placing a small amount of the herb in a glass jar, sealing it tight, then checking for condensation.

5. Store dried herbs in airtight glass or tin containers in a cool, dark location. (Paper is not airtight and plastic can absorb flavors making both of these types of containers unsuitable for storage.

When using dried herbs, a basic rule of thumb to remember is that one tablespoon of fresh herb equals one teaspoon dried herb and 1/3 teaspoon ground herb.

To reconstitute dried herbs, soak in a liquid that will be used in the recipe such as stock, milk, lemon juice, wine, olive oil, or vinegar for 10 minutes to an hour before using.

## HOT PEPPERS ARE NOT FOR THE TIMID PALATE

Why are fiery hot pepper sauces so popular in the tropics? For their cooling effect, of course. Hot peppers—actually the capsaicin they contain—also help to preserve food. This was important in the days before refrigeration.

Hot pepper can be tricky to work with safely. Here are some tips:

1. Watch out! Pepper juice or oil in your eyes may cause considerable pain. Wear gloves while working with hot peppers.

2. The seeds and veins are the hottest part of the pepper. Add or remove them as your taste desires.

3. A whole unbroken pepper cooked in a dish (rice, beans, casserole, etc.), then discarded, will delicately flavor a dish without making it too hot.

4. Adding FRESH peppers to any already prepared sauce will make for some very interesting hot sauces.

5. String peppers together, hang up to dry, and you will have beautiful Christmas tree decorations.

6. Peppers dried in a warm oven, then sealed in a tight jar will keep indefinitely (dry them SLOWLY until crisp.)

7. For best results, grow the plants in pots where they can get both sun and shade. Plant food helps. Use the seeds to grow more plants. Fresh seeds are best, but they will keep if frozen.

8. For different flavors from the same variety of plant, try using the peppers at different stages of ripeness.

Here is a recipe Warren Mauer——who is both a chef and a graphic artist——uses to make a tasty, chunky chutney. He suggests serving it with a grilled fresh fillet of dolphin.

## TOMATO, PEPPER, & JALAPENO CHUTNEY

**4 red bell peppers, seeded and chopped**
**6 cups canned, peeled plum tomatoes**
**3 fresh jalepeno peppers, seeded and chopped**
**1 1/2 teaspoons garlic, finely chopped**
**3/4 cup wine vinegar**
**1/4 cup raspberry vinegar**
**1/4 cup granulated sugar**

Combine all ingredients in a large saucepan. Simmer until softened and slightly thickened. Cool, cover and refrigerate. Makes 8 cups.

Per one tablespoon serving: 4 calories, 0 grams fat, 0 milligrams cholesterol, 19 milligrams sodium.

This is an adaptation of an old West Indian hot pepper sauce that we make at home.

## CHUNKY HOT PEPPER SAUCE

1 medium onion, chopped fine
2 cloves garlic, minced
2 scallions, including green tops, chopped fine
1/4 cup safflower oil
2 stalks celery, chopped fine
1 green pepper, seeded and chopped fine
3 small Scotch Bonnet peppers, seeded and minced (or any
   chili pepper)
2 medium carrots, peeled and grated fine
8 large ripe tomatoes, peeled, seeded and chopped fine
1 teaspoon ground cloves
1 sprig fresh thyme or 1/4 teaspoon dried thyme
1 cup red wine
salt and pepper to taste

In a skillet, saute onion, garlic and scallions in oil until vegetables are tender yet not browned. Add celery, green pepper, Scotch Bonnet peppers and carrots. Cook until vegetables are soft. Add tomatoes, cloves, thyme, salt and black ground pepper. Continue cooking, stirring occasionally, for about 45 minutes until ingredients thicken. Add red wine. Cook for another 10 minutes on low heat. Cool. Store in a glass jar in refrigerator. Makes 2 cups. Per tablespoon, it has 31 calories, 2 grams fat, 0 milligrams cholesterol and 20 milligrams sodium.

## A WORD ABOUT NUTRITION

Each of the recipes contained in this cookbook have been analyzed for their calorie, fat, cholesterol, and sodium content. These four nutrients are those which many people are concerned about limiting in their diet due to their association with increased risk for major health disorders like diabetes mellitus, high blood pressure, heart disease, and cancer.

Prudent daily recommended intakes of these nutrients for adults, according to national nutrition groups, is as follows:

Calories:    Men           ---- 2400 to 2700 /day
                 Women      ---- 1800 to 2000 /day

Fat:         Thirty percent of total calorie intake. For men this translates into 80 to 90 grams per day. For women this translates into 60 to 65 grams per day.

Cholesterol: 300 milligrams daily. For sodium: 2,000 to 3,000 milligrams daily.

## DIETARY GUIDELINES

These guidelines, formulated by nationally recognized nutrition professionals, offer sound advice for healthy eating. They do not, however, address the special nutrient needs of persons who have specific health disorders. For these special dietary needs, seek the advice of a registered dietitian.

1. Eat a variety of food. A balanced intake of fresh fruit and vegetables, whole-grain breads and cereals, milk and dairy products, and protein foods like lean meat, poultry and fish is the best way to assure achieving all nutritional needs.

2. Achieve and maintain a desirable weight. Control

overeating by eating slowly, taking smaller portions, and avoiding second servings. Make regular exercise a part of every day.

3. Avoid foods brimming with fat, saturated fat, and cholesterol. Substitute fish and poultry for red meat. Substitute low-fat milk or cheese for their regular counterparts. Use margarine in place of butter.

4. Eat foods rich in complex carbohydrates and fiber. Fiber is the indigestible part of plant foods that contributes to good digestive health. Whole-grains, fresh fruits, and vegetables are an excellent source of both complex carbohydrates and fiber.

5. Shake the salt habit. Enjoy the natural flavor of foods, or season with fresh herbs and spices. Steer clear of salt-laden processed foods such as cured meats, salted snack crackers, chips, canned soups and condiments like catsup, mustard, olives and pickles.

6. Avoid excess sugar. Use less of all sugars including white and brown sugar, raw sugar, honey, jam and jelly. Replace cakes, cookies, pies and ice cream with fresh fruit for dessert. When shopping, avoid products with ingredients ending in "ose" in the top five listing. Sucrose, maltose, glucose and dextrose are all words for sugar.

7. Last, if you drink alcohol, do so in moderation.

Reference for Nutrient Analysis Information: Each recipe was computer analyzed by the Nutritionist IV nutritional accounting program. This program is produced by N-Squared Computing, Salem, Oregon. Additional information was supplied by: Food Composition Tables for use in the English-speaking Caribbean.

## INDEX